C000194777

The Maze & the Arc of Light

The Maze & The Arc of Light

A Journey with a Purpose

Hope Tod

Findhorn Press

Copyright © 1989 Hope Tod
First published in 1989 in a limited edition by Link Up Publishing
Paperback edition first published 1991by Findhorn Press, The Park,
Findhorn, Forres IV36 0TZ, Moray, Scotland

ISBN 0 905249 79 8

All rights reserved. No part of this book may be reproduced, except for quotation or review, without the written permission of the publishers.

Set in Palatino on Macintosh SE
Design and layout by Philip Mielewczyk
Cover illustration copyright © Lawry Gold
Printed and bound by BPCC Wheatons Ltd, Exeter

Printed on 'environmentally friendly' oxygen-bleached paper—no polluting chlorine or acid used in its manufacture.

Do not look at my outward shape
But take what is in my hand

Rumi

Contents

An Introduction by Peter Caddy, Co-Founder of the Findhorn Foundation

Reading *The Maze and the Arc of Light*, I was fascinated to learn that Hope Tod was doing the same kind of work in Somerset that I had been doing in the early days of the Findhorn Foundation, the spiritual community in the north of Scotland. Many of her friends and contacts were known to me and some played an important part in the early development of the Foundation.

I was even more interested to read that one of the discarnate Group with whom Hope Tod is in contact is Robert Ogilvie Crombie, generally known as Roc. At the time when Hope Tod and her group were activating spiritual power centres in West Somerset, Roc and I were doing the same in the Glastonbury area and throughout Britain. We were particularly concerned with linking the Findhorn area, Iona and Glastonbury because we had been told through my wife Eileen that these places formed a triangle of powerful Light centres and that the cleansing of these ancient places of spiritual power was necessary for the anchoring of certain energies for the new age.

We thought we were doing this work alone. It was therefore very exciting to find that similar work was being done by others at the same time.

I first met Roc in Edinburgh where I was giving a series of talks on the Findhorn Foundation. A few weeks later he was brought to the community for a visit.

Roc was a great and wise soul and I found that I had an immediate affinity with him. A learned man, he had been trained as a scientist and had a library of over 8,000 books. Early in his life he had developed a heart complaint which prevented him from taking a permanent job. For years he lived in the country pursuing his interests in science, literature, physics and chemistry and developing a close contact with nature.

He later moved to Edinburgh where he paid frequent visits to the beautiful Botanical Gardens. There, in March 1966, he made his first contact with an elemental being. He saw a beautiful figure, about three feet tall, dancing around a tree about 25 yards away. It was a faun, half human and half animal, with a pointed chin and ears and two little horns on his forehead. His shaggy legs ended in cloven hooves and his skin was honey-coloured. Roc could not believe his eyes.

Later Roc made contact with a being of tremendous power who he realised was Pan.

He appeared to him as depicted in myth, half human and half animal. Although Pan can appear in such a form, he is not restricted to it or to any one place. Pan means 'all' and is a universal energy which is found throughout the whole of nature. Roc was able to respond to Pan without fear; therefore Pan could communicate with him and use him as a mediator between humanity and nature.

On one occasion Pan told Roc: "We are not here to be the slaves of humans, but to collaborate with them to bring about a world of peace, cooperation and brotherly love. A world free from wars and violence. Human disbelief in our existence does not destroy us—it could never do that. We are here and we shall always be here even if the human race destroys itself and this material planet. Humankind is losing its dominion over the other kingdoms with which it shares the Earth by its destructive behaviour, selfishness and stupidity. It is time people looked and saw what they are doing. They must face up to the consequences of their behaviour, which they cannot escape. If they do not, the time will come when only actions will teach them the necessary lessons. By then it may be too late!"

Over the years Roc made many visits to the Findhorn Foundation where he was greatly loved and respected. He was so loving, wise and gentle. As leader of the community, I often turned to him for help and advice. After Roc passed on, there was no contact with him whatsoever. It is only recently that I have become aware, through several sources, of his work on the inner planes. I was therefore very excited to discover this book by Hope Tod and to learn that she has a link with Roc in the work that was done through her and her group.

TIME BEYOND TIME

The bough blossoms. The petals fall.
Time makes no stir, though seasons run.
Day's lantern now, October done,
Prints naked trees on the orchard wall.
On all the wealth that June bestows
Penurious Winter lays his pall.
The golden apples are wizened all.
And the heart dreads what the mind knows.

Yet still, within, the moment glows
In which all time and times are one:
Where blooms the never-withering rose,
And shines undimmed the immortal sun.
New joys and gems his beams disclose.
Time makes no stir, nor seasons run.

Gerald Bullett (1895-1958)

(From Gerald Bullett's book of poems *Windows on a Vanished Time* published by Michael Joseph, London.)

THE SUNFLOWER

Ah sunflower, weary of time,
Who countest the steps of the Sun,
Seeking after that sweet golden clime
Where the traveller's journey is done:

Where the Youth, pined away with desire,
And the pale Virgin, shrouded in snow,
Arise from their graves and aspire
Where my Sunflower wishes to go.

William Blake (1757-1827)

Preface

For as long as I can remember I have been aware that I am on a journey, and on this journey there is one particular place I must go to. And when I eventually reach this place I shall recognise it, and will be able to complete the tasks for which I have undertaken the journey.

It was like entering a large and wondrous Maze where each path I took would lead me forward on my journey or send me back, retracing my steps, to start all over again, until, by trial and error, I finally solved the conundrum of the Great Maze and found myself where I had to be.

This awareness slipped in and out of my consciousness with a teasing insistence, gently urging me on. I accepted it as I would a golden thread, trusting it eventually to lead me to the right place. After travelling for many years to and fro through the Great Maze, I finally reached the appointed place and completed the work. The Golden Thread of Awareness, with its myriad strands, guided me all the way.

Over the years many people have asked me: "How did it all begin and how did you know what to do?"

In an attempt to answer this question I have written these brief glimpses of my long journey through the Great Maze, from early childhood until the completion of the tasks in 1982, which I hope will help people to understand how it all came about.

A complete record of our work with the solar rays is contained in Part Two—'The Arc of Light'—together with the names of all those who took part in the quarterly Light ceremonies and of the Light points we worked with.

May I also suggest to anyone who, having read this book, feels the urge to use our quarterly Light ceremonies and rituals in their own area, to meditate well and ask many questions before undertaking such a task. To work in harmony with the cosmic forces requires much self-discipline, awareness and dedication.

If used incorrectly the rituals could create negative energies which could be harmful to the environment. So do please be very careful, and remember that love, and balance between positive and negative, creates harmony and the awareness of the oneness of all life. True balance is the watchword.

Hope Tod

PART ONE
THE MAZE

PART ONE
THE MAZE

Chapter 1
Childhood and Youth

Early in childhood I decided that physical death for the human being was similar to a snake shedding its skin. On one of our daily country walks I found a complete skin, fragile as tissue paper, on which every mark and indentation of the snake's body was clearly shown. This fragile membrane fascinated me: it was such a complete replica—even the eye sockets were clearly marked. I carried it with great care, admiring its perfection. On our arrival home, I took it to show the gardener: I wanted him to tell me where the snake, who appeared to have slipped out of its skin so completely, had gone. The gardener took the delicate object gently into his hands, looked at it for a while and then grunted. I waited anxiously for an answer to my question. "So you want to know where the snake that was in this skin is now, do you?" I nodded my head in affirmation; so eager was I for the answer that my voice seemed to have deserted me. I nodded again.

"Well," he said, "I don't really know. I expect it's gone off to start a new life; it can do that, now that it's shed its old skin."

This direct and simple answer pleased me very much: it seemed to make such good sense to slip out of your skin and go away to start a new life. My awareness was comforted. Life was a complete pattern and if you followed it all would be well.

At this time in childhood, I became very conscious of the Elemental—the Fairy—Kingdom, and of the pure Spirit of Nature, Pan himself: a wondrous being, full of light and grace, with a tremendous and comforting protective power. When he was close I knew that I was safe.

I was also excited by colour and the way in which it changed the atmosphere around me. I was fascinated by shapes and forms, by the sounds made by natural things, by the sheer wonder and power of earth, air, fire and water. Light was a constant mystery—its ability to change the appearance of quite ordinary things held me in thrall. All the scents and smells of the natural world intrigued me, and my eyes were dazzled by the sun, the moon and the stars: in this infinite space, why couldn't human beings fly like birds? Happily and innocently I basked in all this mysterious energy. As a country child, I soon learned to understand and accept the primal laws of nature—that life lives on life from the insects upwards, each species making its contribution to the whole, enabling the balance and value of each to be blended into a continual creation, a cosmic whole. I had yet to encounter the full force of the unique *homo sapiens* consciousness!

My father was a doctor of medicine and a surgeon in the Royal Navy, where he served his country well and was honoured for his valour. All his life he was very much aware of the elements and their power over humans. He was a great admirer of Einstein and Sir James Jeans, the physicist. In our youth he taught my brother and myself how to sail in small dinghies, taking endless trouble to ensure that we did everything correctly. He taught us self-discipline, patience and a strong respect for, and awe of, the sea, the wind, the sun and the moon. He explained that we were members of the cosmos, part of the whole, and that our cooperation with the natural world would bring us infinite joy, harmony and understanding which, in turn, could be helpful to others. He showed us, by example, the power of spiritual love and compassion.

His sense of humour was delicious! Whatever misfortune befell me, he always managed to make me see the funny side. In his loving presence I felt safe and understood—we seemed to share a common awareness. He had an inner strength which was both formidable and vastly comforting.

My mother was also interested in medicine and the sea. Her medical wisdom was subtle yet gloriously simple and effective. She favoured herbal treatments and really understood the importance of rest and silence, a healing stillness which allowed mind, body and spirit to work in harmony. She had a great love for music and its effect on the psyche. Her musical abilities were well developed—she played with great charm and feeling on the piano and with skill and panache on the violin. Her knowledge of five foreign languages, which she spoke fluently, came from her childhood spent in many different countries as the daughter of a distinguished diplomat.

Gardening and growing plants delighted my mother and we had a large and beautiful garden at our Sussex country house, and a magical orchard. Whilst my elder brother and sister were busy in the schoolroom being taught by our governess, my mother would gently lead me or carry me around the garden and orchard, naming each plant and tree as we reached it so that I could see and sometimes touch it—touching was very important to me. I loved these voyages of discovery which we took together, and the sound of her voice calling out the names of plums, apricots, peaches, nectarines, pears, all of which grew on trees carefully trained and shaped like open fans against the high, grey-stone walls, was like a beautiful invocation to the pure spirit of nature. The scents, shapes and colour of the flowers and vegetables in season were also carefully observed, touched and sniffed at. Especially I loved the mixtures of rosemary, lavender, roses, lilies-of-the-valley, peonies, strawberries, mint, carrot fronds, scarlet runner bean flowers, marigolds in the sun, and the scent of fresh cut grass. They filled my young and sensitive nostrils with pure delight and still linger, hauntingly, to this day.

In spring, the apple blossom in the orchard was a wonder to behold. The sound of bees and insects humming busily about their business of fertilising the blossoms and collecting nectar was a joyful sound which made my ears tingle. I also loved to play with the buttercups shining so brilliantly in the growing green of the orchard grasses. Sometimes we found primroses in fat clumps, their pale yellow flowers reflecting the light, and cowslips with their strong, sweet scent filtering through the pasture. Once we came upon that mysterious wild flower known as the snake's head fritillary; its fairy magic of shape and colour brought me delightful expectations of an unknown elfin kingdom. Although I much admired the cultivated flowers in the garden, the wild flowers in the orchard were still my favourites.

My mother equally shared my father's love of ships and sailing. They owned a yacht which was kept moored in Chichester harbour and on which we spent marvellous holidays, exploring the south coast and anchoring in small harbours where we enjoyed further explorations in the dinghy. It was a simple, idyllic childhood closely linked with the natural world. My mother's religious inclinations were towards Buddhism: serene, gentle, tolerant. Both my parents exercised to the full the precious gifts of compassion and detachment.

***

My maternal grandmother was a very wise person, warm-hearted, friendly and easy to talk to—always ready to listen without interrupting the speaker's flow. Many were grateful to her for this act of kindness and consideration.

We all loved her dearly and often visited her. On our visits we normally conversed with her in French: with her diplomatic and ambassadorial background she knew well the value of speaking many different languages, and always encouraged us, as she had her own children, to speak well with plenty of expression. She deplored the tendency to speak foreign languages in what she called an English accent.

One day I went alone to have lunch with her. We were chattering happily together as we entered the dining room. The table was, as always, most beautifully arranged with sweet-scented flowers, much silver and delicate glass, and many dishes of exciting foods. As we settled ourselves to start the meal one particular dish caught my eye: it was an artistic and lovely blending of yellow and red tomatoes, very finely sliced and decorated with fresh green herbs. As I looked admiringly at the dish, I burst out impulsively: *"O, comme j'adore les tomates!"* Grandmother smiled, and after a short pause, she gently reminded me of what, in my childish greed, I had forgotten. Very slowly, she said: *"Ma cherie, l'on adore que Dieu."* I apologised at once, and then, suddenly, a gush of joy flooded my consciousness. Her words were a key that opened the door to reality and the realisation that religions are all human-made, but the universe is God-given, to be shared freely by all.

This awareness of reality was stunning in its completeness—as years passed it became increasingly clear and answered many puzzling questions—and my joy and excitement at receiving this revelation was such that I eagerly devoured my share of the dish of tomatoes and, to this day, they remain one of my favourite foods. My grandmother was, I'm sure, completely aware of what had taken place—her sensitivity was acute. Her direct and loving simple wisdom was a vital strand in the golden thread of awareness which enabled me to progress through the Great Maze with confidence. My gratitude is with her always.

When my grandmother died, I had such vivid and realistic dreams about her, seeing her as a young woman full of vitality and joy, obviously delighted to be home again with her family and friends. Her smile was radiant and her eyes beckoned me to join in her pleasure, which I did with complete happiness. When I awoke, I was quite sure that, like my snake, my grandmother had shed her old skin completely and was indeed living a new life. This made me so happy for her, and for all of us, that I could not be sad and mournful. Alas, my attitude was misunderstood by one of my aunts who called me a cruel and uncaring child for not weeping at my grandmother's death. Her attitude bewildered me: surely, as I had seen my grandmother so vividly in my dreams, she was infinitely better off there than being an old lady lying in bed in pain and distress?

Slowly, I became aware that many would prefer the sick person to remain alive, no matter how ill they were. This seemed even more odd to me when their religion, which they followed so devoutly, affirmed that, on death, the soul went to heaven, a glorious place of light and joy, vastly superior to life on earth. Then my awareness increased and I realised that those left on earth were really weeping for their own loss, for the alteration in their own pattern of living, for the inevitable confrontation with physical death, and all the fears and doubts that accompany it. So many religions have their dark side, implying that a soul *might* go to hell and damnation if the sins committed in life were too many, or of a certain kind. Thus doubt and faith, joy and fear continually ran through the human mind, tossing the living soul from side to side and all ending up in distress.

I thought about it a lot—all these self-inflicted fears and anxieties puzzled and exhausted me. I had seen my grandmother whole and happy once again, so why didn't they? It would make them so happy and reassure them in their Christian belief of resurrection. I thought of the empty snake skin gently laid aside in the long grasses; all done according to the laws of nature; simply, directly and without the strain of fickle emotions. The animal kingdom seemed to be much more intuitive about life and death, closer to cosmic awareness and eternity.

After my grandmother's death, I went away to boarding school—first a preparatory school in Sussex and then to the pioneer co-educational boarding school Bedales in Hampshire. At once I felt completely at home in its liberal atmosphere, its emphasis on self-discipline and responsibility for others. The freedom we were given was positive and constructive. The school worked as a group—its motto was 'Work of each for the weal of all'.

The atmosphere in the school was, surprisingly for a boarding school, full of eager vitality, enterprise and originality. To the outside world it was known as a 'crank' school and was largely misunderstood, but many intellectual and advanced thinkers, artists, philosophers and musicians were very interested in the new ideas for education of its founder, John Hadon Badley. They could see that co-education in a boarding school could gradually alter the old ideas of segregation and create a more balanced society. School rules were minimal so I soon learned the importance of self-help and cooperation. The school's programming gave us time to think for ourselves. At first it was hard work but equally it was rewarding when a problem was solved satisfactorily. The large number of staff were very generous and wise with their help on all subjects. Music and the arts, as well as academic excellence, were a strong influence on us all. The record of entrants to universities, art schools and music colleges was high in proportion to the school's number of pupils. No school prizes were given. Competition was for excellence and this attitude generated a very high standard, enormous effort and a real pleasure in achievement for its own sake.

As I progressed through the school, my awareness sharpened—I learned the importance of listening carefully, and observation of shapes and forms also became very central to my thinking. Art, music, modern languages and English were my best subjects. Through them perhaps I would find another strand in the golden thread. My musical instrument was the viola and playing it well became terribly important—the sounds were so glorious they filled me with nameless joy and ecstasy. When playing in the school orchestra I experienced the wonder of harmony and unity. Tennis was the only game I found myself able to play with skill and real enjoyment. I was placed in the First Six at the age of 13. Others in the team were either seniors or prefects.

My love of being outdoors, close to the earth, led me to choose outdoor work instead of lacrosse and cricket. We all had duties to perform helping in the school gardens and on the farm. I learned to hand-milk cows, make butter, dig trenches, hoe the vegetables, turn and carry the hay, and many other useful occupations. My instinct urged me to keep close to nature, as though through the natural world the task I had to accomplish would be revealed to me. This awareness gave me great comfort.

When I was fourteen and a half, I suffered a serious accident in the school quad. It was a wet afternoon so we were playing indoor rounders. I ran, slipped, and as I fell hit my head very hard on the bannister of the staircase leading to an upstairs classroom, causing me to fall on my face on the concrete floor of the quadrangle. I was badly concussed and had to remain quiet in a darkened room for a week. I remembered nothing of the event: afterwards the school Matron told me I had walked down to the sanatorium with a mistress and apologised to her for causing a disturbance. (My subconscious, well trained in the ways of diplomacy, must have taken over!) This accident, however, altered me in a very interesting way. I became much more conscious of, and felt much closer to, the elemental world of wild nature. I listened to the wind, watched shadows moving across a field; wild flowers began once again to fascinate me, their beauty and their fragrance reviving old memories—but what old memories?

At fifteen and three quarters I developed rheumatic fever. We were enjoying a summer holiday on the yacht when the fever started. I was taken home and put to bed, and there I remained for six months. The fever fluctuated and the intense pain exhausted me. It was an endurance test for my mind as well as my body. Slowly I recovered my physical strength, a long hard struggle requiring much self-discipline and a great deal of patience. The after-effects of the illness remained with me, dogging my footsteps time and time again with what the medical men call post-clinical symptoms. Once again my awareness was heightened: I concentrated on drawing and painting and it seemed to fill my whole existence. Through my imagination my hand was becoming skilled in creating designs and patterns which delighted and surprised me. This experience filled me with joy and renewed energy. Endless possibilities began to loom—the journey was becoming exciting once more.

When I left Bedales, my parents suggested I should extend my study of Art and Design. I was offered the opportunity of going to the Arts & Crafts School in Frankfurt-am-Main. The idea excited me so I accepted it without much thought. I had never been to Germany before! I brushed up my conversational German before setting off solo by train and cross-channel steamer, and since we had often travelled to the continent before, it was not a new experience. I was to be met at Frankfurt station by members of the Paquet family, who were known to my parents, and I would stay with them in their house in Wolfgang Strasse, whilst I attended the Arts & Crafts School, which one of their six children already went to. The father of the family, Alfons Paquet, was the Editor of the *Frankfurter Allgemeine Zeitung*, a well-known German newspaper. Marie Paquet, the mother, was a professional painter with her own studio in the Old Town. They were a fascinating family with two boys and four girls.

They all lived at home whilst studying various subjects such as arts, music, drama and science. It was a large and happy household full of activity, especially in the evenings when music was played, stories were read out and dramatic episodes enacted. The current paintings and designs were also displayed and discussed. The whole family made me very welcome and I looked forward to making good progress, as well as having fun.

However, the underlying Nazi influence soon began to disorient me. Everyone urged me to take no notice and insisted that everything was all right, but it definitely was not. I kept on feeling an undercurrent of subtle manipulation, effected with such cunning it was difficult to define. But when several Jewish students at the School started disappearing and no one wanted to say what had happened to them except that the State had 'intervened' and it was none of their business, I became really alarmed. Were they all hiding their fears with wild parties and good time fun? "We're all right," they would say as they sang their loud and cheerful songs in the packed beer-cellars, sitting on long benches, arms linked, swaying to the music and drinking from huge mugs on the trestle tables in front of them. It all seemed to be such a jolly, carefree scene, but I was completely bewildered. It was almost as if I could see clearly what they could not—all those gentle and joyful young souls who were so interested in the arts and eager to express their talents were being unwittingly sucked into an awful situation quite against their better judgement. They were too trusting, too innocent, too happy. I found it impossible to concentrate, and much as I admired their ability to work in such an atmosphere, I could not. My thoughts and feelings were constantly jarred by sights and sounds in the town and the school. With great sadness—and a presentiment for their future—I decided to return to Sussex.

The following year, my friend Katherine Armfield and I went to Paris, she to study the viola, and I to work in an art academy. We shared an upstairs room in a small hotel in the Latin Quarter. The elderly concierge was like a character from one of Victor Hugo's novels. She took a keen interest in all our comings and goings and was extremely good at recording messages received on her ancient telephone.

The atmosphere of Paris, light and easy, the familiar language, the music and the cafes, all lifted my spirits and tuned my thoughts to a delicate pitch of enjoyment. I began to work with a will and found endless subjects to fill my sketch books. The Luxembourg Gardens were particularly beautiful, and the true spirits of nature danced with delight among the chestnut trees, the vivid flowers and the deep, mysterious shrubberies.

We became acquainted with many artists, among them Ossip Zadkin, the 'White Russian' sculptor, well known and much loved by the bohemians. He introduced us to many of his friends. The Lapique Perrins and the Jolie-Curie families, already scientists of fame for their cancer research—as well as many musicians and artists—welcomed us. We enjoyed picnics in the Bois de Boulogne and beside the river Seine. We were often joined by Catlin Macnamara (who later married Dylan Thomas). She was studying 'Isadora Duncan' dance in a nearby studio and was having money problems. We helped her as often as we could.

In the Latin Quarter, Kay and I became known as 'the two angels' because we wore bright copper snoods in our long hair, which in my case was very curly. Kay's was straight and very blond. We also wore flowing skirts and capes. Oh, how we enjoyed ourselves!

When not working we visited art galleries, gazed at classical buildings, rummaged through endless book stalls on the left bank of the Seine. We sat on wooden benches and watched the crowds, taking in every detail of their appearance. Some were real gypsies, others smart Parisiennes. We walked for miles and found small open markets in forgotten squares. In one a group of young men played on small bagpipes. Their music was hauntingly beautiful, bringing back the atmosphere of old France and the Troubadours. We also attended evening concerts, seated high up in the gods, a score of the music being performed laid across our knees so as not to miss a note. We even climbed the Eiffel Tower.

This period of my life was a wonderfully happy one. My spirits soared and I became increasingly intuitive and aware of the power of thought. It was indeed a joyful path through a part of the Maze—one I shall always remember with pleasure.

On returning to England, I decided that I would like to go to the Central School of Arts & Crafts in Southampton Row, London, to train as a textile designer and illustrator. I hoped this would enable me to earn my living whilst doing what I loved so much. I made the necessary application and was granted an interview. With me I took a portfolio of drawings and designs to be looked over by the principal. To my delight, I was accepted as a student.

Before I went to the Central School of Arts & Crafts, however, I had the great good fortune to meet the well-known poet, essayist and novelist, Gerald Bullett. He lived not far from our home in Sussex, and often drove over for morning coffee and to join in the general conversation. My parents kept 'open house' and there was always a largish number of friends calling in to enjoy this most civilised pastime. Although Gerald was over 20 years my senior, his quiet manner and vivid imagination attracted me. Instinctively, I knew that he would answer my endless questions and that I could learn from his quiet wisdom, his sensitivity and his sudden bursts of bubbling humour. Our mutual attraction to words and their meaning, the magic of nature and the surrounding downland, led us to take long country walks together. There was one particular favourite known as the Sickle Path: it started near Gerald's home, the Old Farm, East Harting, and from there went gently up the hill, first straight and then in a long curve to Phyllis Wood. At the edge of the wood, high on the downland, a wonderful panorama of the surrounding countryside came into view. Continuing through Phyllis Wood, and then across a small clearing, the path finally ended up at a tiny public house known locally as 'Hooksway' (the Sussex vernacular for a sickle being a hook). Here we could enjoy a well-earned rest, and a meal of bread, cheese and pickled onions, accompanied by a mug of Henly & Constable's best ale (brewed in Chichester), served outside on trestle tables on the tiny lawn, overlooking a pond alive with multi-coloured ducks, and shaded by large and sturdy oak trees. In this rural setting we were completely at peace. Gerald talked, and I listened intently. His grasp of metaphysics, which he expressed so wisely, and our mutual love of the natural world, drew us close together into a magic circle of our own creation. Gerald said we were companions on the Path, sharing the mystery of the South Downs, and that this would always be so. The phrase he used was kindred spirits. We also talked often about poetry and poets, a subject very close to his heart as it was to mine. His admiration for the artist and poet William Blake was boundless, as one of his books—*The English Mystics*—clearly reveals. Gerald heightened my awareness of the profound truth expressed by William Blake in his short poem entitled 'Eternity':

He who binds to himself a joy
Does the winged life destroy:
But he who kisses the joy as it flies
Lives in eternity's sun rise.

This poem remains to this day one of the strongest strands in my Golden Thread. Its philosophy is timeless.

Gerald endowed me with so much of his love, his sense of wonder and his gentle humour. He confirmed and shared my heightened awareness of life on earth and of eternity. He comforted my human heart with wise and loving words and actions. Our earthly union was brief in time but complete in essence. It enabled me to progress through the Maze with renewed strength and determination.

***

One autumn afternoon, I made my way to my brother Dick's rooms in New Court, St John's College, Cambridge. I had come up from Sussex to make arrangements for the Medical Society Ball shortly to be held in the Dorothy Cafe. My brother, who was reading medicine, was eager to make up a party, with me helping by bringing some of my girl friends as partners for him and his friends. We were chatting together over a cup of tea in his sitting room when two of his college friends dropped in. They were introduced to me as Alex Slater and Dudley Tod, and were obviously very good friends. Alex was a warm-hearted, cheerful extrovert, full of easy banter, amusing jokes and quick laughter. Dudley was a lowland Scot with family roots deep in the soil of Ayrshire and Dumfriesshire. He was extremely tall, with the longest legs I had ever seen. He had golden-brown hair, blue eyes and an appalling stammer which he tried to control with endless patience. His helpless smile when he struggled to speak was so gentle and charming. I was immediately impressed by his quiet determination to overcome his cruel affliction.

As we sat together, I vaguely sensed something familiar about him. It was like a faint memory of someone I had known long ago, like meeting again with an old acquaintance after a prolonged absence. It teased my senses but no clear answer came . . . and yet his silent recognition and understanding linked us together from some forgotten time. I don't know why, but as we sat together, I sighed several times, then I felt a quiet conviction that here was an old acquaintance come to keep me company and help me on the journey. We smiled at one another.

Very soon we became close friends, drawn together by a shared memory from a distant past. After he graduated with an honours degree in economics, and before he left England to start his career in a large, long-established mercantile firm in Madras, South India, his family decided to give him a farewell party. He invited me to be his partner for the event. It was a marvellous occasion, where aunts, uncles, cousins and other relatives all gathered to join in the fun, which started with a visit to the Savoy Theatre. This was followed by dinner and dancing at the Savoy Hotel on that amazing raised dance floor which vibrated and swayed when it became too full of dancers. On the following morning we all trooped off to Victoria Station to see him off and wish him God-speed on his long journey to India via the port of Marseilles.

Dudley and I did not see each other again until January 1945. The outbreak of the Second World War kept us apart but we did correspond regularly and persistently. During these years Dudley left his firm to go on active service with the 410th Gurkha Regiment to which he had been drafted and commissioned as an officer. In spite of all the horrors and disruptions of a world war, including the censor, our letters got through, sometimes taking months instead of weeks and days. They were all carefully numbered and none went missing. They were like a slender bridge of words spanning the distance between us, and their arrival was indeed a miracle of human determination amidst the difficulties of war. Meanwhile, my training at the Central School of Arts and Crafts in Southampton Row was progressing well: all the various aspects of design fascinated me. I attended classes in still life, book illustration, costume design, posters and textile design. All these subjects interested me but finally I decided to concentrate on the course in textile design which included both woven and printed textiles. The various techniques and methods of production dating from ancient times fascinated me. I came to love the feel of all sorts of different materials, from fine silk to thick woollen, and to see how the designs, structured for them, flowed and rippled across and through them creating magical effects of light and colour.

I made regular visits to the Victoria & Albert Museum to study the old methods of production—hardblock, screen and cylinder printing. I loved the atmosphere of the museum: it was very creative, with all the various officials courteous and helpful. Their knowledge of their subject was inspiring and nothing was too much trouble once they saw that someone was really interested and anxious to learn. When handling the old tools used by former craftsmen, I would get a clear impression of these people and how they used their implements. I seemed to slip into a time warp and was often startled when a fellow student made a remark which brought me back to the present. How skilled these early craftsmen and women must have been; how dedicated and careful they were to produce wonderful results with such simple instruments. With few worldly distractions they were able to put all their energy and imagination into the creation of beautiful designs—producing superb and complicated patterns by close observation of the natural world all around them. It was this creative energy which I seemed to pick up and was surrounded by when handling their tools and implements. It was very exciting—almost intoxicating. New ideas for designs seemed to flow into my consciousness and I could hardly wait to return to the studio to start working them out on paper.

After a year's study, and a great deal of practical application, I started cutting my own blocks and printing a variety of materials with my own designs. All went wonderfully well—so well in fact that I decided to hold a small exhibition of my finished work. It was a success and the materials sold well. It also brought in a number of orders. I was so very busy completing them, looking forward to the future with Dudley's first home leave from India, when the hounds of war were unleashed in Europe. Hitler's Germany had finally committed the unforgivable crime of man's inhumanity to man, and as a result the rest of the world would have to suffer and die. The Second World War was declared, and overnight all the people I had met in Germany, including the kind and loving Paquet family, had become our enemies. It was both mind-boggling and terrifying, and also chilling proof of what I had experienced so strongly during my time at the Frankfurt Arts & Crafts School, which had finally driven me home to Sussex filled with a sense of foreboding for the future of these innocent and loving people.

Automatically, I completed my orders and delivered the printed materials to their purchasers. That done, I left the studio and, without hesitation, joined the Women's Land Army. I had always been aware that working with earth, air, fire and water and cooperating with the natural world was the ideal way of living but, alas, the complex *homo sapiens*, the supreme predator, craves the excitement of danger—even to the destruction of his own kind. He plays political games which turn into unimaginable horrors, whipped up by fanatical hysteria, greed and envy, leading to appalling slaughter and destruction which finally overcome him and all around him. The whole history of humankind is littered with these terrible events, seemingly undertaken with complete disregard for the dignity and the sacredness of all life.

During the six years of world-wide warfare, I worked on the land and with animals. I was continually impressed by their dignity and willingness to help humankind and by their acceptance of our foolish and sometimes very cruel ways. Their instinctive understanding of our language and tone of voice filled me with admiration. I greatly appreciated the friendly companionship of the horses when working with them, sometimes for long periods of ploughing, drilling and harvesting, when a close rapport could build up between us. All the horses and cows I worked with became my close friends and I loved them dearly. The barnyard hens and the pigs in their cosy sties were also extremely intelligent about their own way of life—each understood their own status quite clearly. The animal kingdom is filled with wise and extraordinary beings who tolerate the curious activities of humankind with infinite patience and acceptance. They often made me feel ashamed of myself and my fellow humans.

When the long day's work was done, I rested. Often my body was very tired but my mind was active so I read from Chaucer's *Canterbury Tales*, Virgil's *The Georgics*, and the works of WH Hudson, Richard Jeffries and Mary Webb. 'The Land', a long and beautiful narrative poem by Vita Sackville-West, which she completed in Persia in 1926, and Henry David Thoreau's *Walden, or Life in the Woods*, helped me to balance the horrors of war heard daily on the radio and to realise that the true and lasting values which exist before and after wars, and which eventually overcome evil ways and thoughts, are eternal.

The farms I worked on were in Sussex, Kent and Hampshire, and we too had our share of horrors: bombs frequently exploding all around us, aerial battles raging overhead, with 'planes falling to earth in flames and dead or wounded pilots often found in nearby fields and woods. Several times when bringing in the cows for early morning milking I was 'sniped at' by low-flying enemy aircraft returning to base after a night raid on one of our cities. We endured many land mines which terrified the animals, the ground shaking and erupting beneath their feet with the force of the explosion. These huge gaping holes in the landscape and the death and destruction they caused were quite appalling. Finally, we had the robot V-bombs catapulted across the Channel by the German forces in occupied Europe. Waiting for the engine to cut out and knowing that the explosion would be close was a chilling experience. I had two near misses—each time landing in a deep ditch, flat on my back!

In January 1945, Dudley came home on compassionate leave. He had been in India and on active service with his Gurkha Regiment without home leave for nine years. His troop ship docked at Liverpool on the 9th after a hazardous journey in close convoy from Bombay.

Our long-delayed reunion was to take place at Dudley's godmother's house in Chelsea. I had obtained weekend leave from the farmer I was then working for in Hampshire. It was truly wonderful to be together again and after the first few hours the years of separation melted away. Our regular correspondence had indeed been a firm bridge. Meanwhile, war-weary and battered London took us to its heart: we enjoyed dining and dancing at the Savoy Hotel and walking in Battersea Park, still green and peaceful in spite of all the bombs.

On March 3rd we were married in St Jude's Church, South Kensington, by special licence. We chose London because so many of our families and friends were living, were posted, or were on leave in London at that time. Train journeys to Sussex might have been difficult and perhaps delayed by enemy action. We all reached St Jude's Church safely but halfway through the marriage ceremony the air raid sirens blared out their warning of approaching enemy bombers. A quick decision had to be made. Dudley and I looked at one another and then we nodded to the vicar performing the ceremony to continue. After several loud bangs some distance away, the long all-clear sounded. We were well and truly married.

The reception was held at 4 Cheyne Walk, Chelsea. A large and quite beautifully decorated wedding cake dominated the centre table—I was amazed by its three tiers and all their intricate decorations. It looked most impressive but when Dudley drew his *kukri* to cut the cake, an alert waiter slipped forward and deftly removed the three tiers, all made of cardboard, and there on a platter remained a tiny fruit cake. Wartime rations were then at their lowest!

We spent the first three days of our honeymoon at the Savoy Hotel. On our wedding night, a large land mine fell in Hyde Park blowing out most of the windows of the Cumberland Hotel. The remainder of our honeymoon was spent in Cambridge: we travelled by train from King's Cross complete with our bicycles in the guard's van. Dudley had arranged for us to stay with one of his old landladies who had looked after him when he was an undergraduate. Her name was Mrs Bennett and she looked after us beautifully in her trim little terraced house. She was obviously pleased to see Dudley again and told me what a nice young man he was, no trouble at all to look after. When I mentioned our nine years' wait to get married because of the war, her comment was: "Coo, I call that broth warmed up!"

We cycled for miles in and around Cambridge, entranced by our freedom in the open air, the lovely familiar landscape and the sheer joy of being together at last. One morning we walked into the Porter's Lodge at St John's College. The head porter looked up from his desk, then smiled holding out his hand and said: "Hello, Mr Tod!" It was a marvellous moment: after nine years and a world war, he had immediately recognised Dudley. We visited Dudley's old rooms in New Court, also my brother's old rooms close by in the same Court. We strolled along the Backs and over the Bridge of Sighs. We attended evensong in St John's Chapel and visited Dudley's tutor.

We also spent a very long time in Heffer's Bookshop where, among other things, we bought a lovely print of a water-colour painting by Charles Knight entitled 'Ditchling Beacon'. It was so cool and serene with a small pond in the foreground and the Ditchling Beacon standing out clearly against an azure blue sky. It conveyed so vividly the atmosphere of the bare South Downs, and as soon as we saw it I knew we must purchase it. Later on in India, its cool serenity became very precious to me—it was so calm and beautiful. I must have spent many long hours admiring it. It continually beckoned me and became almost like an icon. Only years later, when we lived in the converted potting shed near the pond at the foot of Ditchling Beacon, did I fully understand why I had been so drawn to this painting. It had simply been another strand in the Golden Thread of Awareness.

All too soon Dudley's compassionate leave came to an end. On May 1st 1945 he was flown back to India in a Sunderland flying-boat, which left from Poole harbour in Dorset. The European war was drawing to a swift close: all was action and haste. Soon I would be joining Dudley—it would involve a very long sea journey on my own, and the responsibility for all our heavy baggage. Undaunted, I started on the exacting task.

Chapter 2
Venture to India

For my journey to India, I was booked to travel to Bombay on the s.s. 'Burma', a very small cargo ship belonging to the Paddy Henderson Line based in Glasgow, and due to sail from Greenock, a River Clyde port on the west coast of Scotland.

Before my sailing date arrived, the European war came to an end, but the Far Eastern conflict rumbled on. At the appointed time, when a fixed sailing date was decided, I made the journey from Sussex to Glasgow in a variety of trains and taxis. The nine large pieces of luggage I had with me consisted of packing cases containing our wedding presents and all that was necessary for our new home in South India. I had a very anxious time counting these cases on and off the trains during the journey to Glasgow until I finally saw them disappear safely into the hold of the s.s. 'Burma'.

There were only thirty passengers on board and half of them left at Port Said. I shared a cabin with Olive Turner who was travelling to India to get married. We soon formed a friendly shipboard group and with all the wartime 'blackouts' lifted, the first part of the journey was easy and pleasant. Our first port of call was Port Said, where we spent two days unloading cargo, so we all went ashore sightseeing and walking along the banks of the Suez Canal, overshadowed by the huge statue of De Lesseps, its builder. Our second stop was Port Sudan where we had another two days, during which time our little ship was refuelled with coal—our means of propulsion coming from its coal-fired boilers. At Aden we stopped once more for three days to take on fresh cargo. Again, we all went ashore during the daytime, exploring the fringes of the Arabian Desert. Finally, from Aden across to Bombay, we were completely 'blacked-out' again and travelled in close convoy to avoid enemy action. We were back in a war zone, but thankfully the powers operating in the Arabian Sea were kind to us and we landed safely in Bombay harbour.

Once again the nine pieces of luggage had to be transported, this time from the harbour to the station via the customs house. I managed with the help of two kindly officials and many chattering coolies, all of them seemingly eager to get me on the train safely, together with all the baggage intact.

My first sight of the Madras mail train was very exciting: it stood in the station like an enormous caterpillar stretching down the line into infinity. Its sheer size was awe-inspiring, and the huge steam engine, with a large 'cowcatcher' grid in front, was being prepared for the journey. Tiny figures ran around it like ants around their queen, while from the giant itself smoke and hissing steam erupted, filling the air with tiny droplets of water and soot. The heat and smell of oil and grease which assaulted our nostrils seemed to fill the station with excitement and a sense of urgency. Officials and passengers hurried along the platform looking for reservation tickets stuck onto the carriage windows. I had been allocated a single coupe which consisted of a bunk bed, a table, a wash-basin and a lavatory. I was delighted and soon had my bedding roll laid out and my food in its various containers placed on the table beside my thermos flask of cold water.

The journey to Madras was a long one—two days and two nights. I was excited at the thought of crossing the Indian continent from Bombay in the west to Madras on the east coast, travelling all the way in a steam train, and I settled into my single compartment to enjoy this unique experience. As the great engine pulled slowly out of Bombay, I realised that the roof was covered with 'hobo' travellers clinging on for dear life. I could hear them pattering about overhead and talking to one another, and this continued all the way to the outskirts of Madras.

The vastness of India was impressed upon me as we travelled endlessly through an empty landscape, or occasionally thundered through a small station. I saw very few people in this great open country—the vast population seemed to have been drawn as though by magnets to the big cities. The gregariousness of these human beings puzzled and amazed me as I sat by myself watching the scenery flash past. My solo journey from Sussex to South India had so far taken me just over three weeks, and this fascinating experience with all its strange and interesting encounters came to a happy ending as the great mail train drew gently into Madras station, where I saw Dudley waiting for me on the platform.

When the War Office had flown Dudley back to India after his compassionate leave, they had arranged that he should be seconded from his Gurkha regiment to Madras harbour to organise and control the refuelling of the coal-fired ships which called there before making their non-stop journey on to the far-eastern war zone. These ships were vital to the 'big push' which our war machine was organising to try and end hostilities still raging further east. Thus, Dudley was at the Harbour Office all hours of the day and night; he also had to visit ships at anchor in the harbour to ensure they had their full complement of coal to make a safe journey into dangerous areas. Some of the captains told him hair-raising stories of near misses, or their problems with engine failures, but these sturdy little Merchant Navy ships always seemed to find a way out, even to the extent of firing the ship's engines with ward-room furniture!

I did not see very much of Dudley when I first arrived in Madras. His work in the harbour was almost non-stop, so I volunteered for daily duty serving meals, tea and cool drinks in a YMCA canteen catering for the troops passing through Madras. These soldiers loved talking about their homes and their families, and photographs were quickly produced for me to admire and comment upon. I could sense their longing to return to familiar faces and known landscapes. They never spoke about their experiences on active service—it was always about home, girl friends, wives or children. One day, when I had mislaid the tin opener, a huge African soldier quietly took the tin of condensed milk out of my hand and rapidly opened it with his teeth, handing it back to me with an angelic smile.

This state of affairs continued until World War Two ended abruptly with the atom bomb being dropped on two cities in Japan. Six appalling years of worldwide inhumanity had been endured, and we were all stunned and exhausted by so much carnage. With the end of hostilities, Dudley returned to his civilian job with Messrs Parry & Co Ltd, Madras, as Manager of their Shipping & Transport Department.

The great heat in Madras was made just bearable by the humid atmosphere. The old saying that 'Madras is nine months hot and three months hotter' was certainly correct. After six weeks, though, one's body seemed to adapt itself and the heat became less noticeable. Dudley and I lived in a small ground-floor flat in one of the old houses surrounded by a big garden. Our flat consisted of a large central room—a combined dining and living room—on each side of which was a bedroom and a bathroom. The bathrooms had a concrete floor sloping slightly towards a hole in the outside wall, into which the water drained when one tipped up the tin bath after use. Hot and cold water came in buckets brought to the door by the waterman who heated it in a large copper in the garden by building a fire underneath it with wood and any odd thing which needed burning. With rain only once in three years, this process worked very well. The lavatory in the bathroom was merely a bucket, with a wooden lavatory seat across the top. Beside this 'thunderbox', as it was known, stood a smaller bucket full of sand to sprinkle into the lavatory bucket after use. When tipping up the tin bath, one always had to be careful to avoid the bucket of sand!

All our food was cooked in a separate building known as a 'godown' which stood a few yards away from the back of the house. The food was then carried to a 'hot box' which stood on the wide back verandah. From this 'hot box' which was heated by a small charcoal brazier, the butler carried the food to our table in the large central room.

In a climate so reliable and predictable, living conditions were simple and easy. The wide verandahs kept the inside rooms cool with the help of large ceiling fans, built like aeroplane propellers, which worked day and night using a very small amount of electricity. We had to employ a large number of servants because the Indian caste system, whereby each servant only did one job according to their caste, was very much in effect: the sweeper swept, the cook cooked, the butler waited on us, the waterman carried and heated the water, the gardener gardened and so on. They each came and went—doing their job and then disappearing again. Some lived in the 'godown', others came daily. Only the butler was about most of the day and snoozed happily on the back verandah. I found this simple easy-going life quite delightful and well suited to the intense heat. Each day the butler, the cook and I arranged the menu. The cook then went to market to purchase the food required. I had a large store cupboard (locked) and from this I doled out the various dry ingredients like sugar, rice or flour. Every morning I gave the servants a cup of coffee and a rice cake which they consumed with much laughter and giggles—I always enjoyed this little ceremony. Sometimes the 'egg lady', with her large flat basket filled with eggs, which she hawked about the house, would join us. A cow or a buffalo was also brought daily to the back verandah, led by its owner, who milked it directly into a jug as I watched. Fresh milk indeed!

Sounds in Madras were clear and quite extraordinary—each sound came clearly into the house through the mesh-covered windows and the wide doors opening directly onto the verandahs. Indian voices calling to one another in the clear air, laughing and scolding, were like a Greek chorus surrounding my day. We were all living close to the earth, content with simple things and natural ways.

The perfume of South India was spicy and pungent—in this hot climate many of the flowers had thick, waxy petals, their leaves were bright green and very glossy, and their scents were powerfully sweet. Marigolds, the flowers of the sun, grew everywhere and their brilliance against the blue sky was a sight to behold. In our garden we had a huge border of marigolds, salvias—bright red with dense green foliage—coloured cosmos and exotic cannas. Tobacco plants grew under our bedroom window to scent the evening air. Bougainvillaea, frangipani and other scented climbers crept over every wall and fence and trellis, creating a sweet-smelling and dramatically coloured 'backcloth' to the garden. These old Madras gardens, designed and planted years ago by merchants and their wives, contained many beaufitul and useful trees, such as tamarind and breadfruit, now grown to full maturity and yielding large crops. But danger also lingered: there were ants who devoured all before them and there were snakes and lizards and many poisonous flies always on the look-out for possible victims. One day the gardener found a five-foot cobra curled up and basking in the sun on top of the garden wall. Scorpions were also a daily hazard, both inside the house and in the garden.

A short while after he had rejoined his civilian firm, Dudley was sent by them to supervise and organise the unloading of American grain ships in the little coastal harbour of Tuticorin.

The grain was a post-war gift to India from the USA. As the unloading would take several weeks, I was invited to join Dudley. It was a very interesting and amusing experience, which included a fascinating and quite unexpected discovery for me.

As the American ships approached Tuticorin, the Harbour Master realised they would be far too big to enter the harbour for unloading. They would have to lie at anchor outside the harbour and all the discharging would have to be into lighters —shallow draughted barges—which would not only increase the cost but also the time of unloading. The Harbour Master began to panic but Dudley in his quiet and efficient way overcame this and reorganised all the difficulties so that unloading progressed smoothly and the American ships' captains accepted the situation.

To the best of our ability we entertained the captains and crews when they came ashore, arranging parties and visits to local places of interest. In return, they invited us to visit one of their grain ships to look around and have a meal. After touring the ship and admiring the luxurious quarters they all occupied, we were invited to step into the captain's cabin to enjoy some American hospitality. The cabin was superb and the menu placed in front of us with a flourish was more than impressive. Every single item came out of the ship's cold store: nothing had been bought ashore, not even vegetables or fruit; their self-sufficiency was absolute. The meal was delicious and their coffee beyond praise. Dudley enjoyed his rye whiskey as much as I did their cool fresh orange drinks.

During our stay in Tuticorin we visited the Tuticorin Club regularly and met many of the local people. In the main clubroom I found a small 'cupboard library' of English books—about fifty in all. Looking through them, I discovered a copy of one of Gerald Bullett's novels, *A Man of Forty*. It brought my old friend vividly into my consciousness and made me realise how the written word links us together. It was another strand in the Golden Thread of Awareness. This unexpected discovery in a tiny club in South India fascinated me and filled my heart with renewed energy and gratitude.

When we returned to Madras, I was offered the job of 'Secretary to the Room of Women's Work' at the Victorian Technical Institute in Mount Road. It was a very grand title for a large craft shop which acted as an agent for 52 different missions of all denominations scattered around the area—some far out in the presidency in very isolated places. The missions employed local women and trained them to create the most beautiful and intricate embroidery, lace, drawn thread work, children's clothes, underwear and soft toys. All the work was sent to us in Mount Road where we checked and priced it, and then displayed the items for the general public to buy. Each month we sent off the money for goods sold, taking a small commission to cover our expenses. One Methodist mission produced fascinating woven material which they made up into shoulder bags, table mats and counterpanes. We worked hard at our display of their products and made very good sales—I was sometimes amazed at the amount of money we sent out each month. As secretary I was responsible for two Indian clerks (book-keeper and typist) and two Anglo-Indian girl assistants who worked in the shop.

In the other half of the craft shop was all the men's work: mostly wood carvings, ivory figurines, basket work, *papier maché* articles all elaborately painted, and many other crafts. The men's section was run by a delightful Indian who was himself very artistic and full of a flair for display, and together we all made a good team, with our clerks, assistants and other helpers. I liked working with Indians. On some occasions I was the only European present and blended in quite naturally, listening and taking part in unity with them. I learned a lot and made many good friendships.

It didn't surprise me, for example, when some of the older Indian women came and talked to me about medicinal herbs and the merits of various oils and spices. These quiet and gentle women in their lovely saris, which rustled with every movement, were intuitive and sensitive. They lived close to the soil of India and they understood its rhythm. Hindus love the natural world and appreciate and value the fruits of the earth. I felt a close link with these women and willingly shared with them my own thoughts on herbs and spices and oriental oils.

One year I was invited to give some talks on design and abstract art to an invited audience in the Madras Museum. The audience were mostly Indian and proved to be both alert and questioning. These talks led me to be invited to exhibit with the South Indian Society of Painters, and at one such exhibition I won first prize in the Design section. I also completed and sold a large number of textile designs to Benny's Mills, one of the large cotton manufacturers in South India.

Another interest at this time was a drawing and painting class I started for young children. I also designed both Christmas and greeting cards. Through my association with the Victoria Technical Institute, I became involved with the Madras Handloom Weavers, an entirely Indian organisation. We had great fun experimenting with new colour combinations and patterns. Actually two of the weavers were Persian and their amazing natural skill in weaving was, I am sure, due to inherited ability from past generations. Similarly, the traditional music of South India interested me greatly: I attended many concerts where the *Ragas* were played and expressed with superb sensitivity. Indian dance forms with their long history of dedication and perfection were also thrilling to watch, becoming quite mesmeric as they advanced to a climax. I felt a close and powerful affinity with all Indian art and music, and it was a very joyful path I travelled with them through the Maze. But, instinctively, I knew it was just a fascinating part of the journey to be cherished and remembered as I progressed towards where I must go.

The majority of the Madras population are Hindu. One day I was invited to the Hindu wedding of a friend's daughter and it transported me into another world. The wedding took place in the bride's home which was transformed for the occasion into a magical chamber filled with music, coloured lights and a central stage, tiny in size , but just large enough for the bride and groom to sit on and to be slightly raised above the surrounding guests. A variety of symbolic display abounded, with oranges and marigolds featuring strongly. We sat for hours during the ceremony and afterwards for the feasting, with hundreds of little food dishes of an infinite variety being passed around. The costumes worn by the chief 'performers', if I may call them that, were very elaborate, almost Mogul in style and appearance. Thick silks and brocades mingled with the bare chests of the men and the muslin saris worn by the young girls. Heady scents filled the air and everyone, including the men, wore flowers in their hair and around their necks. I was thrice garlanded with sweet-scented flowers and presented with an orange.

The Hindu belief in reincarnation strengthened my own

beliefs; it made sense of so much that was questionable in other faiths and religions. It also made me more than ever aware that religions are human-made but the universe is God-given. This realisation which came to me in childhood through my grandmother's quietly spoken words, was with the passing years being constantly confirmed and strengthened.

When it was very hot we often visited the beach at Adyar to swim in the Bay of Bengal and enjoy the cool winds and clean sands. To reach the beach we walked along a track which was very green, overgrown and sweetly scented by wild flowers. It ran close to the boundary of the Theosophical Society's grounds; it was upon this beach that 'Bishop' Leadbeater, one of the founders of the Theosophical Society, first saw Jiddu Krishnamurti playing with his brothers and immediately proclaimed him 'The New Messiah'—a title which Krishnamurti eventually rejected to follow his own wisdom and understanding. It was a very beautiful stretch of coastline known locally as the Coromandel Coast. We found it an entrancing place in which to have a quiet evening picnic: the moonlight, the sound of the surf pounding on the beach, the vastness of the starlit sky and the restless sea all combined to create an atmosphere of continual movement taking place in an ordered universe completely untouched by humankind. We were as grains of sand in the cosmos, in harmony with creation and part of the whole.

One year we flew from Madras to Colombo to stay with Dudley's friend WJ Childeston (Childy), who was the manager of the tea estates known as the Balangoda Group, Bogowantalawa. These estates lay like an emerald green carpet on the foothills of Adam's Peak and were known as 'Childy's Kingdom', because not only was he the area magistrate, the rationing officer and the controller of the tea factory, but also the superintendent of the wonderfully modern hospital and maternity wing which also belonged to the Group. Childy was a very gentle but firm man who spoke Tamil fluently and also the local dialects. He ran his 'kingdom' with infinite patience, tolerance and wisdom. We were given a wonderful welcome when we arrived at his bungalow. His cook, known as Mr Punch because of his long and curving nose, had spent days preparing all sorts of elaborate dishes to tempt and delight us. We were allowed to wander about the estate and Childy took us to beauty spots and on a conducted tour around the tea factory and the hospital.

When Childy made his tours of inspection of the tea gardens, he always rode on a pure white Arab horse and was accompanied by his two white Pekinese dogs named Fatty and Mimi. As he cantered through the tea gardens, the mane and the long tail of his Arab steed flowed out like pennants in the breeze, whilst the two little Pekinese dogs also had their tails flying as they raced along keeping up with the horse and the rider. They all made a glorious sight as they moved across the wide landscape. This brilliant cavalcade, conspicuous for miles around, was Childy's deliberate way of warning the plantation workers of the master's approach. It also made for quick identification at times of an emergency or accident.

Childy's household was very self-sufficient. There was a large flock of poultry in the big yard. The vegetable garden was enormous, very carefully cultivated and full of delicious produce. He also had a house cow which had cost him a lot of money. He told me he was very disappointed by the milk yield as he felt sure it should be more than the one bucketful the cowman brought to the house each day. I offered to milk her and she yielded one and three-quarters buckets of milk. The cowman insisted that the cow, which was an English shorthorn, had been generous to me because I was an English lady! My own guess was that three-quarters of a bucket daily found its way into the home of the cowman and his friends as a useful bargaining commodity, and although Childy rather ruefully agreed with me, we decided not to say anything. As if by some miracle, however, the following day the cowman brought one and a half buckets of milk to the house. Childy smiled at the man, saying, "This is excellent, the yield has increased. The English lady has put a good spell on the cow!" And so the little drama was happily resolved. The cowman now knew he could no longer hold back three-quarters but just one quarter of a bucket. In this way, no one had lost face because the master had said it was the English lady's good spell that had increased the yield. Such was an example of Childy's wise understanding of the rural mentality and the need for dignity in his kingdom. By gently tempering their greed, he achieved a balance which everyone understood and respected.

The flower garden of the Balangoda Bungalow fascinated me.

Daffodils and primroses flowered happily side by side with Michaelmas daisies and autumn crocus. Roses, tulips, delphiniums and wallflowers made exotic displays in the wide floral borders. There seemed to be no seasons of spring, summer, autumn and winter—everything planted just grew, flowered and then faded, in one long sequence. The lawns were lush and green, shrubs grew thick and climbers and vines occupied every bit of spare place on walls and buildings. It was rather like a glimpse of paradise. The views from the gardens were fantastic. Mountains and valleys created a continuously changing panorama, with tea gardens like green oases scattered amongst them. We were indeed close to the sky and, very occasionally, on a really clear day, we could see the top of Adam's Peak, the highest mountain in the area.

The road to Bogawantalawa was a wide track through the forest, where the high trees were filled with little fawn-coloured monkeys continually chattering to one another and swinging from branch to branch like expert circus performers. Some were quite tame, often swinging down to take a good look at us as we walked along. If we scattered a few bananas around they came down helter-skelter, snatched the bananas and started eating them as they swung back to safety in the high branches. At the edge of the forest and not far off the track were several deep pools of shining black volcanic rock filled to the brim with very clear and bitterly cold water which flowed in from a stream higher up. These pools were held in awe by the local inhabitants of Bogawantalawa—they were so deep and the sides so slippery, that only in one or two places was it possible to enter the water and return safely. Here we bathed and had picnics, but always our senses were heightened by feelings of danger and excitement. At one pool, the water ran over the edge dropping onto a precipice thousands of feet below. We had to be careful not to get too close to the edge of this one! The sound of the falling water and the fine spray it created filled the air around the pools creating a magical effect which thrilled and delighted me. It was one of the most wild and dramatic places I had ever been to. Nature spirits abounded—they gave us a cautious welcome and we never over-stepped their hospitality. It was such a beautiful place I could have stayed there for the rest of my life. Bogawantalawa—'Childy's Kingdom'—was a paradise on Earth and we were very privileged to enter such a place in the 20th century. We saw the Earth in its natural splendour and wild state, undisturbed by its inhabitants who worked in harmony with nature and who had, at that time, no desire to exploit it for material gain.

It was difficult to leave such splendour and natural delight. Sadly I kissed Fatty and Mimi and said a tearful farewell to Childy and his 'kingdom', reluctant to continue my journey through the 20th century Maze. But gradually my awareness was growing that the place I was destined to go to was in Europe and not in the East. It steadily became stronger, overriding all my interests and curiosity about life in India and the East.

India in its ever-changing state was a fascinating but terrifying kaleidoscope of events and experiences. We travelled around a great deal, from north to south, east to west, absorbing all the wonders and cruelties of this vast continent. We watched the change from empire to independence and all that this involved. It reminded me of going to boarding school after having lived at home: so many changes took place, with loyalties becoming divided and attitudes hardening. Nationalism took pride of place, tinged inevitably with feelings of revenge and accusation. It was a traumatic time for all of us as we tried to balance hot and often violent emotions with cool reason and good common sense, a task invariably difficult for gregarious and quick-tempered human beings of whatever race or colour. It was the everlasting problem of give and take, the endless lesson we all try to learn and express so that harmony and goodwill can prevail. Its infinite permutations fill the world with sorrow and joy.

Chapter 3
The Sussex Downland and the Warren

In July 1956 Dudley was appointed to the London office of his company, to be in charge of their shipping and transport arrangements and to work with their broker on the Baltic Exchange. Meanwhile, the company's main office in Madras and their many factories and branches all over India were slowly becoming Indianised.

The company's London office was situated in 13 St James's Square, a beautiful and historic part of London's West End. Dudley was delighted to find himself working in such elegant and spacious surroundings. We decided to find ourselves some rented accommodation in Sussex as the company had kindly offered to pay Dudley's train fares. We tried various places and finally settled near Ditchling, Dudley commuting to London five days a week from nearby Hassocks Station.

The accommodation I found was one half of a large converted potting shed standing in the grounds of the one-time East Sussex Agricultural College at Westmeston, which lay at the foot of Ditchling Beacon. As soon as I saw it, I recognised that it was the original site of the Charles Knight painting we had bought on our honeymoon in Cambridge and which had become my cool icon during the hot years in India. Oh, the wonder of the Golden Thread and its myriad strands! The property was owned by a widow whose husband had recently died. She lived in one half of the converted potting shed and we had the other. Our half consisted of a large central living room with an open fireplace, one bedroom, one kitchen and a bathroom and wc. The layout was similar to that of a Highland croft, very cosy and comfortable to live in. We also had a garage to ourselves and a large garden. The setting was completely rural, overlooking fields and woodlands. The approach to this unusual dwelling was down a farm trackway off Underhill Lane, which ran along the foot of the downs from Westmeston to Clayton. Underhill Lane, according to HJ Massingham, the author of many books on rural England, is one of the oldest lanes in the country.

Our half of the converted potting shed was most aptly named 'Peterscroft'. (On the local map the field in which it stood was called Petersfield). Living at the foot of Ditchling Beacon and 'within my icon' was an amazing experience: the painting and the landscape joined up in my vision, creating a feeling of intense joy and renewed energy. It was a good omen.

Dudley was soon comfortably settled into his routine of five days' commuting to London and two days in the country. Meanwhile, I cycled into Ditchling to do our household shopping and also discovered that the Southdown Bus Company ran a service through Westmeston into Lewes, the county town, which proved most useful to me. In Lewes, I found a huge non-fiction library in a large three-storeyed house in St Ann's Crescent. It was an enormous building, each floor stuffed with miles of shelves and what seemed like millions of books. To me it was a veritable treasurehouse of books on every subject I was interested in, and from then on I travelled into Lewes every week to wander through this fabulous storehouse of the written word. It never failed me—I learned so much, enjoyed myself so much and it was all free!

One morning at the Westmeston bus stop I met Mrs Maimee Howard who lived at St John's Cottage, Westmeston. She was also a regular visitor to the Lewes non-fiction library. We soon became good friends, visiting each other regularly to take tea and talk. She was a fascinating person, born and brought up in the Cape Province of South Africa. Her father had been the editor of the 'Cape Times' and her knowledge of Africa and the various tribes was most impressive. She had travelled all over South Africa and spoke the native languages fluently—a fact which enabled her to visit and understand the inhabitants of towns and villages remote from western civilisation. Her main interest was world history and I learned a great deal from this interesting woman who had travelled the world and knew how to talk about it. Sitting in her quiet room, surrounded by its curious and unusual objects, was like being in a time capsule with a wide viewfinder. As she talked, vivid pictures flashed into and across my vision. Some were so powerful and clear I seemed actually to be in the country concerned, among the people, seeing them move around and hearing them talk. Whenever Mrs Howard stopped talking and suggested tea, I was always startled to find myself sitting in her cottage at the foot of the South Downs in Sussex. These journeys to far lands stimulated my inner vision, filling me with a new sense of wonder at the vastness of the planet.

After that first meeting at the bus stop, every time Mrs Howard went abroad, whether to Italy, Greece, Turkey, Spain, Syria, Egypt, Persia, Samarkand, Russia or India, she always brought me back a small gift from each country as well as telling me her wonderful traveller's tales. These little gifts are still my touchstones, happily reminding me of a truly remarkable woman who really understood human beings and all their devious ways. Her tolerance and her gentle laughter at humanity's absurdities was a valuable lesson, indicating the importance of balance, serenity and true perspective.

Our landlady, the owner of the converted potting shed, was also a very kind person. Her mother had nicknamed her Sam and this had remained with her all her life, mainly because she detested her first name of Muriel. Her great interests were gardening, the occult and driving her car. Very early on in our friendship, I was invited to join her in going to meetings, lectures and seances. The lectures were on esoteric subjects and often very interesting and informative. The meetings, however, were a different matter—everyone attending them seemed to have a particular subject which they wished to expound upon with the hope of converting as many people as possible to their way of thinking. I found myself longing to be alone in the open air, just listening to the sounds from the natural world—the real world!

The seances, held in dark, stuffy rooms with closed doors and windows, gave me a feeling of being trapped. I longed to see the light of day come streaming through the closely-drawn curtains. I realised it was a method of communication which brought help and comfort to very many people, but it was not for me. My interests lay with the plants and trees, with the animals all around us, with the elements and all their powerful energies, and the effect they had on the planet.

Quite often I experienced feelings of great excitement as if the paths through the Maze were becoming shorter and wider; more directly oriented towards the exit where I could find the single path leading to the appointed place. But where was this place? Why was I so stupid and seemingly unable to understand? At times it really was alarmingly like being caught in a very small maze-within-a-maze with no way through. And yet my life was full of love, joy and new friendships—so full there never seemed to be time enough. Were there perhaps too many interests? Was I being too self-indulgent? Not listening enough to my inner consciousness? Shouldn't I think less and listen more?

With these kinds of thoughts in mind, I decided to take regular walks by myself through the fields and woods—just walking and listening. During these walks, I discovered a wonderful thing: if I stood very still in one place and closed my eyes, a great calmness came to me, as though the spirit of place was being revealed. My awareness became heightened; I felt intensely alive. I could sense the earth's energy beneath my feet and I knew, without any shadow of a doubt, that I was progressing, albeit very slowly, towards the right place. It was all a matter of timing and faith and not trying too hard. I also found that this power was much stronger out of doors, when I was surrounded by the elements. This knowledge strengthened my instinct that the work I had to do would be done out of doors and in harmony with the cosmic forces. Living so close to the earth in our converted potting shed and surrounded by fields and woods enabled me to rediscover my awareness of the nature kingdoms and the elemental kingdom which I had found so very real and joyful in my early childhood.

After we had been neighbours for a year, our landlady, Sam, came to me in great excitement. She had been reading a book on 'automatic writing' and was very keen to try it out. Would I be willing to try it with her? I said I would experiment with her, but I was not willing to go into a trance, even if I could. We sat at her table and Sam explained that we must sit quietly with a blank sheet of paper in front of us and a pen in our hand, awaiting results. I insisted that before we started we should say a prayer of protection, which we did. After sitting quietly for a long while, I wrote a few sentences but did not feel it was 'automatic writing' as expressed in the book because I was holding the pen and in control of its movement. To me it seemed as if shapes and forms were being transposed into words by my own awareness and what I had written did not seem to have any real value at all. I viewed the experiment with extreme caution and decided not to try again, but I was at least interested to realise I could do it. Perhaps if it was used under controlled conditions, for a specific purpose, and with great care and self-discipline, it could be beneficial in bringing through information where no other way was possible or suitable.

The experiment with Sam taught me to be careful but not blinkered. Many responsible people have used this method to help others and increase knowledge. It reminded me of Morse Code and the way it had proved to be so valuable for very many years. All kinds of methods, if used seriously and with great care and attention, can be of infinite use as links in the chain of communication.

In Lewes I found many books in the non-fiction library written by Juliette de Bairacli Levy, a unique herbalist, traveller and writer. She pioneered herbal treatment for farm animals as well as domestic pets. Her book *The Herbal Handbook for Farm and Stable* is particularly well-known. Her work, with Sir Albert Howard's approval, in treating sheep had very far-reaching effects. Juliette sold her various herbal remedies through a postal service, so I decided to write to her through her publishers, Faber & Faber in London, requesting them to pass my letter on to her wherever she might be. Her reply came from an Arab house on the shores of Lake Galilee where she was then living and collecting herbs.

Juliette wrote that her herbalist friend Olive Wilson, who lived on the Godshill Ridge in the New Forest, was her agent in England and orders could be sent to her. I wrote to Olive Wilson and ordered herbal teas, wild garlic tablets and honey from the Spanish mountain area where rosemary bushes grew in abundance and the bees feasted on them giving the honey the most delicious flavour. My order arrived promptly and enclosed with it was a warm and friendly letter from Olive Wilson informing me that she had two friends living at Burgess Hill, just the other side of Ditchling Common. She added that she had written to them suggesting they came to visit me. These two friends proved to be Eileen who taught handicrafts to disabled people in their own homes, and Jane who taught at a girls' school in Burgess Hill. They lived together in an old farm cottage in a field beside the Keymer Road, in a very sunny and open position, with long views towards Wolstanbury Hill. Both were keenly interested in arcane subjects, herbs and healing. Jane wrote poems and short stories centred on the New Forest and in later years I did a number of pen and ink illustrations to accompany some of these.

She was also a member of the World Spiritual Council which had its headquarters in Tunbridge Wells. It was, in fact, the British Section of the 'Conseil Spirituel Mondial'—an organisation founded in Belgium in 1946 under the patronage of Queen Elizabeth of Belgium and listed among the non-governmental departments of the United Nations Organisation. Non-denominational in outlook, it sought to unite men and women of goodwill so that together they could work towards solutions for human problems without abandoning their own convictions. It was not an enterprise dedicated to conversion but to collaboration and sought to establish the basic unity of various philosophies and cultures, arts and sciences, both from East and West. It recognised that goodwill was the active principle of brotherhood and the root of peace.

Jane invited me to go with her to a meeting of the WSC in Tunbridge Wells with the idea of becoming a member, and I gladly accepted. I found the members very interesting people with wide horizons, great knowledge and tolerance. The meeting was held in the Quaker (the Friends) Meeting House, and many Quakers were active members as were many of other denominations, from both East and West. I was very much drawn to this society of goodwill that had branches in so many European countries, including Holland, France, Denmark, Belgium and Great Britain. Regular conferences were held at the Spa Hotel, Tunbridge Wells. Dudley and I both eventually joined the society and soon found ourselves on the committee with people like Roland and Dorothy Northover, Sir George Trevelyan, Mr Mung Ming Ji, Mr M Tufail (Imam of Shah Jehan Mosque near Woking), the Rev AB Cote and many others. My fluent French came in very useful when the Paris contingent came to the Spa Hotel conference and I spent many happy and instructive hours as interpreter. Through our membership with the WSC we also met Margaret Forbes, the Scottish artist and poet, who became one of our most beloved friends.

Margaret had a studio flat in Burgess Hill. Her oil paintings were powerful, beautifully executed in subtle colours with cosmic energy bursting out of them as they revealed the miracles of the natural world. Some people called them abstract, but to me they embodied all the majesty and wonder of Planet Earth. Colour, light and movement swirled through them, rewarding the viewer at each fresh look with some new aspect or a different dimension. They were indeed awe-inspiring. Margaret was also a skilled portrait artist, and her pencil drawings were quite exquisite. Her poems, like her paintings, were strong, subtle, full of cosmic awareness as well as earthly reality, and all were beautifully crafted by her sensitive imagination. She was a person who loved and understood the silence. Her paintings have been regularly exhibited in many well-known galleries in England and Scotland. Private collectors also treasure her work.

I visited Margaret regularly to listen to the fascinating stories of her studio life in London, her short and unsuccessful marriage to a naval officer and her long and rewarding friendship with Stanley Casson, a well-known archaeologist, writer and lecturer. They both loved Greece and the wonderful light in that part of the Mediterranean. Her descriptions of their visits to various islands, as well as Delphi, were fascinating. Margaret also had a long connection with India: her Forbes grandfather had been a High Court judge in Bombay, with one of the city's streets named after him. He was also a gifted water-colour artist. She herself had been born in the Bombay area but had been brought home to Scotland while still a young girl. Her interest in India was reflected in her lifelong membership of the Sri Aurobindo Society, whose ashram is at Pondicherry in South India. Margaret also studied at the Arcane School in London with Alice Bailey. The Buddhist Society was a great interest of hers too. Their magazine *The Middle Way* was edited for many years by a great friend of hers, Clare Cameron, who worked with Sir Christmas Humphreys, the president, before moving on to become editor of *The Science of Thought Review*, a very popular philosophical magazine founded by HTH (Harry Thomas Hamlin) which came into being in Bosham House near Chichester in West Sussex.

I first met Clare Cameron in Margaret's studio in Burgess Hill and was immediately drawn to this vivacious person. There was a quality about her, a gentle and determined strength of purpose, which had overcome so many difficulties and problems in her own life as well as the lives of others. Her great love of words also linked us together. Clare's poems—and she had written a great many—were both sensitive and very perceptive, full of a love of nature and spiritual values. Her prose writings and her grasp of the real world were impressive. I admired her various publications and gradually collected them all. Whenever Clare came to visit us, her conversation was always fascinating and covered many subjects. I was particularly interested in her opinions about the Buddhist faith.

As time passed, our circle of local friends grew and grew. All of us seemed to have an interest in various aspects of healing, so I decided to start an absent healing group in a small outbuilding in our garden. Many friends, including our landlady Sam, came regularly, bringing with them the names of those in need of help. The energy they brought, combined with the love and understanding which flowed from them, was very powerful for good. Their self-discipline and balance enabled us to channel through our meditations much spiritual strength and help to those in need. It was all beautifully simple—furthermore, I am sure we ourselves received as much grace and healing as we channelled to others through our prayers and our meditations. As in all things spiritual, it was indeed the case that, as you give, so you receive.

One fine day, eager to join our little absent healing group, came Miss Kay Poulton, who was at that time living with her friend Mrs Evelyn Peat in Ditchling. I was delighted to meet her, as I had heard from others about her interest in absent healing. Her visit was quite a long one. She loved to talk and I listened with increasing interest. It transpired that Kay's passion was the theatre. During her life she had been secretary and general helper to Lilian Baylis at the Old Vic. She had also been personal secretary to Sir Lewis Casson, the actor/manager and founder member of the Arts Council. Kay had also developed a great interest in esoteric teachings and had studied long and hard with the Theosophical Society in London. Her fund of knowledge on so many different subjects was most interesting. Soon she was visiting us regularly to share our meals and, because she was such a good speaker, she kept us all listening intently to her amazing adventures and stories about all the famous people she had met. Her keen sense of humour and her descriptive powers gave us endless amusement and made us laugh until our sides ached.

Kay had a penetrating and questioning mind. She was very good at research, filling notebooks with careful comments on her chosen subjects, with all the facts and figures carefully listed. She was a well-trained secretary but, to my surprise, at times I noticed that she lacked self-confidence regarding her personal life and showed some confusion about the past, as if uncertain about various events and in need of some help. At the time she was collecting material for a book she planned to write about her experiences. These were events which had taken place in the past for which she longed to find more confirmation, but those able to supply it were all now dead. I gathered also that she had a lot of questions she wanted to put to them, if only she could find a clear channel. Previously, I had mentioned to her my one experiment in 'automatic writing' with our landlady, Sam, and she must have reflected on this, for one day she asked me quite directly if I would be willing to try again, this time on her behalf.

It was a direct question requiring a similarly direct answer, and I thought about it carefully and calmly for several days. I realised it would be a very serious undertaking and a responsibility needing great care and self-discipline. It had to be positive and serve a definite purpose. That had been my instinct when I first tried the writing and had then stopped because as far as I could see there was no definite purpose being served. But now Kay's request for help had come directly to me and fell completely into this category. Moreover, I had faith in her integrity. I argued that if I could use this gift of 'transposed writing' to help others increase their understanding and awareness of the oneness of all creation and the reality of eternity, then this effort of mine would be worthwhile.

I decided to try once more, this time on Kay's behalf. Into my consciousness came the words 'As ye sow, so shall ye reap'. When the time was right, I sat down at the big table in our living room to prepare myself. In front of me I had several sheets of blank paper and in my right hand I held my pen. After saying my prayers of protection and affirmation, I listened in complete silence with my eyes closed. My concentration became one-pointed, cutting out all external thoughts so that the energy, the *fohat*, could flow uninterrupted into my consciousness. The shape, colour and form of a sentence, coming to me on a vibration, needed all my concentrated attention. A tingling like a mild electric shock ran down my arm, a sentence formed in my consciousness and I wrote it down carefully, still with my eyes closed so as not to break the concentration. The first words and those that came after read as follows:

"We greet you. We do not come to bring a new teaching. The world is already full of teachings. We are members of your own group who are willing to try and answer serious questions from those on Earth who are in real need. The reply will be according to the question asked. We are *not* fortune tellers! We come for a particular purpose. The effort of writing this is very great and is not undertaken lightly by us here or by you on Earth. If willing, you will be our scribe 'Golden One', so called because like us you are attached to work which is connected to the solar ray. You are indeed a suitable medium for the pen. We thank you. Teacher."

So, apparently, transposed writing *was* part of my incarnation work. I agreed to undertake it to the best of my ability. From then onwards all messages would start with 'We greet you' and end with the signature 'Teacher'. This puzzled me because the very first message received indicated they had not come to bring a new teaching. So I asked why the messages were signed like this and learned that 'Teacher' acted as a 'Keeper of the Gate' and this name represented the responsibility of controlling and helping those who came to answer questions or make suggestions. Free will always had to be paramount. The whole process was carefully balanced so that harmony and goodwill as well as a respect for the feelings and the privacy of all concerned was not abused or violated. When giving a message or a suggestion, the names of those involved would be given. Some might sign their own name or mention the earthly name of the one to whom they were writing.

It is difficult to express my feelings regarding this information. I was aware of the two-way contact but I needed to be absolutely sure in my own mind, so I asked the Teacher the following question: "Is all this coming from my own imagination? Am I simply making it all up?" The tingling in my arm grew more noticeable; I could feel the *fohat* being increased. The reply to my question came through with great strength as follows:

"No, Golden One, it is *not* all coming from your own imagination. You are *not* simply making it all up. You flatter yourself if you think that! It is a form of communication which uses your imagination to enable the words to be written on paper as you are now doing. We give you shapes, forms, symbols and colours. Your heightened awareness interprets them into words and your imagination makes sense of the words. You then write the words on paper for others to read. I am myself a member of your group in eternity. Like the others here I live in my etheric body, therefore I am an amalgamation of many different characters and personalities, all controlled by the One Spirit—my Higher Self. We are all like this. With no need for physical nourishment as you need on Earth for your mortal body, we are free to follow our true interests and talents.

We also have duties and tasks to perform for the well-being of all life—because life is eternal. You are my task! At other times I follow my love of painting with the brush and writing with the brush. Poetry, music, love of colours, shapes and forms, light on water, landscapes and the close study of wild flowers and herbs fill me with delight, and these delights I share with you. Rhythm and sound in all life is fascinating to listen to and watch. This we also share. These interests link us together.

On Earth the character one undertakes for a particular experience is polarised and one often feels shut out, isolated, unable to complete the task single handed. Many people experience this. But if *contact* is made, as you have done with your pen, then continuity takes place. Thoughts and words are blended in harmony and unity, bringing much joy and feelings of achievement. All becomes part of the whole. Our etheric bodies blend, communicate and build up a rapport which we can *all* share.

Now do you understand? I am not just one person but the essence of so many who all love you. Work with love and love will work with you. Teacher."

Such a powerful and beautifully worded answer to my question reassured me. I felt safe and knew I would be protected whenever I undertook the transposed writing. As I became more experienced in this work, I found I could write with my eyes open and still hold my concentration. Practice improved and speeded up the whole process but it always had to be done with self-discipline and extreme care. It was a gift to be used with love and precision and absolutely no liberties must ever be taken. At first Kay sent me written questions and I sat in silence, said my prayers and read the questions out loud, then picked up my pen and awaited the answers. As they came through my consciousness, I wrote them down. From the first, they were polite, thoughtful and remarkably pertinent. Kay found them very helpful and reassuring, although sometimes they directly contradicted her ideas and opinions, but on our researching further the subject she was concerned about at that time, their answer proved to be correct.

After a while Kay brought her questions to me herself, sometimes ten or twelve at a time. We sat together, Kay on my right so that she could read the answers as they came through and ask the next question without having to talk to me. In this way, my own consciousness remained clear and uninterrupted. The sentences came through so quickly I was always amazed that my written words made such good sense when we read them through after the session. The replies to Kay's questions about the early Greek theatre, the actors and their techniques and stage craft, were quite fascinating. I learned a lot from these sessions on so many different subjects. Kay also received many relevant messages from her father and various close friends who were anxious to help with confirmations and explanations of past events. Her cousin Max, killed in the 1914-18 war, was particularly helpful and supportive, bringing her much joy and relief. They had been very close in childhood and in their teenage years.

Eventually Kay's book was published, the title *Harvest of Light* being suggested by the question-and-answer group and gladly accepted by her.

On several occasions I received messages without asking any

questions. These communications were usually urgent and precise, giving information in a few cryptic words. The first one I received quite appalled me. It said: "Olive Wilson is dying on her feet." It was a great shock and I wondered why it was given to me. Was it true? I had to test the veracity of the message in some way, so I rang Jane, Olive's friend, and in a roundabout way I enquired how Olive was. After all, her recent letters to me had been full of plans and ideas about her future work of building up a new herbarium, of her long walks in the New Forest, her children and grandchildren, as well as a lot of amusing gossip. There was a very long pause on the telephone line and then Jane said: "Olive is very ill—cancer of the spine has been diagnosed but she wants to carry on as normal for as long as possible and doesn't want surgery. Her actual words were: 'I want to keep on my feet, busy collecting herbs.'" Jane's voice broke into a sob. After a second she continued: "Oh, Hope, I am completely shattered. Olive is my beloved friend. I just don't know how I will manage when she is gone. Please help me."

I tried to give Jane all the sympathy and love I could muster, encouraging her to talk it through. Poor Jane—it was a very bleak outlook for her. Olive had been like a mother to her and Jane's visits to the New Forest were the highlights of her year. I visited Jane several times and let her just talk about Olive and I think that helped her most. The message I had received had been correct in all its stark simplicity, and I felt humble and awestruck as well as very heavy-hearted. This gift was indeed a great responsibility. Within six months Olive was dead.

On another occasion the message was equally stark and direct. Dudley's mother was a patient in the Convent Nursing Home on Ditchling Common and had been there for just over two years, constantly passing the time with reading and writing letters—she had a large and varied correspondence covering half the globe! I visited her once a week and we both went to see her on alternate weekends. The nuns were very kind and gave her every attention. Friends and relatives occasionally came to visit her, taking tea at her bedside and having a good long chat over past events. Suddenly I received one day, completely unexpected, the following stark message: "Muriel Tod's days are numbered." I was alarmed and went straight away to the nursing home and rang the bell. Sister Anthony opened the door and said: "Oh, Mrs Tod, I was just going to telephone you. Your mother-in-law has had an embolism." Quietly I went into mother-in-law's room and saw her lying in bed in a slightly twisted position. I greeted her lovingly and she managed a small smile and added a few words.

Sister Anthony was such a kind and wise soul, I felt my mother-in-law was in safe and understanding hands which would gently guide her out of life in a balanced and loving way. A week later she died from another stroke at the age of 88. On the morning she died, just before I awoke, I had a vivid dream. I was in her room at the nursing home; Sister Anthony was praying beside her bed, in which mother-in-law lay completely covered by a long counterpane. Suddenly the counterpane was thrown back and a tall young girl arose quickly from the bed and ran out of the room, her long blond hair streaming out behind her. I awoke with a start, wondering where I was. An hour later the Reverend Mother telephoned to say that mother-in-law had died early that morning. It reminded me very much of my grandmother's death and I knew that my mother-in-law was all right. She had shed her old skin and gone to a new life.

As all these stark and direct messages were given to me personally, I never divulged them. I tried simply to help those concerned to the best of my ability. I record these two incidents long after they actually took place so that the reader may appreciate the kind of responsibility transposed writing imposes on the receiver. Mercifully, I have not had too many of these 'direct statement' messages, but their truthfulness did enable me to comfort and assist those concerned. For over 25 years dozens and dozens of people, from all walks of life, have sent me questions or come to visit me bringing their questions with them. In some cases the postal aspects of this work are very revealing. Some send stamped, addressed envelopes; some do not. Some acknowledge receipt of the messages and send their thanks; others do not! I have never advertised or made a charge for this exacting work and have always accepted that this gift must be used with love for those in need who ask the questions. It is such a precious link with eternity.

***

One bright and sunny morning in the summer of 1961, Mrs Howard telephoned me suggesting we cycle over to Danny House, Hurstpierpoint, to visit one of the last E-type Elizabethan mansions to be built in the country. It was their official open day so I immediately accepted the invitation. Her suggestion excited me but I did not quite know why, apart from the fact that I am always interested in visiting old houses and experiencing their atmosphere.

We set off early in the afternoon on our bicycles, travelling along Underhill Lane to Clayton where, after crossing the main Brighton-to-Hayward's-Heath road, we continued along New Way Lane which ran from the Matsfield Arms Public House at the foot of Clayton Hill all the way to Hurstpierpoint. It was a very narrow lane with high banks and many undulations, and just before it merged into the Hurstpierpoint Road were the main gates of Danny House. As they were open, we cycled straight through and across the park towards the magnificent house, so beautifully set in the landscape with the rolling South Downs as a dramatic backcloth. Far away in the distance we could see Chanctonbury Ring, and close behind the house rose the height of Wolstanbury Hill, with both Clayton Hill and the Ditchling Beacon clearly visible not far away.

We were given a most interesting guided tour of the ground floor of the house, with its great hall, library and many reception rooms. The owners, the Campion family, were not in residence and had let the property on a long lease to the Mutual Householders Association. On our return journey homewards along New Lane, I noticed a little farmhouse at the end of a long chalk track. Just below the farmhouse was an enormous Sussex barn with great double doors on either side. I let out a cry of delight as I pointed it out to my companion. Quickly, we jumped off our bicycles, pushing them against the bank, and stood still gazing upwards at the sight. The chalk track led up to the top of Wolstanbury Hill. The small farmhouse nestling on the side of the hill was an early Tudor building with one very high chimney stack which stood up like a fantail. Fat boxwood hedges surrounded the garden which sloped down to the fields below. It was a dwelling with the most beautiful setting I had ever seen. Impulsively, I turned to Mrs Howard and said, "That is where I would like to live—it's a magical place." She agreed and suggested that it must belong to the Danny Estate.

After a while, and still in a very thoughtful mood, we slowly pushed our cycles up the long rise in the lane. Reaching the top, we stood still and looked back. The little farmhouse was bathed in soft light, and the green beechwoods surrounding it in a half moon were like a green cloak of protection. The crown of Wolstanbury Hill, high above us, shimmered in the late afternoon light. A gentle breeze fluttered the air around us. Birds were singing their evening songs and the cows in the field below the farmhouse grazed peacefully. This scene spread out before me was so beautifully tranquil yet so full of natural energy that I began to wonder if perhaps this *was* the appointed place. Standing quite still, I closed my eyes.

Immediately, I felt the spirit of the place drawing me to itself like a magnet. Then I knew something important would happen to me here, but I must be willing to wait until the time was right. A calm certainty surrounded me the moment I inwardly agreed to wait. I opened my eyes; the tranquil scene was unchanged and the natural energy still vibrated.

After a moment or two we mounted our bicycles and pedalled home in the warm evening air. When we parted at the end of my trackway, I must have seemed rather preoccupied because Mrs Howard, with a smile on her face, said, "I do believe that little farmhouse has enchanted you."

"Yes," I told her, "it has and I'm so glad it has happened."

"I am glad too," she replied, kissing me goodnight. Suddenly I felt so tired, I just wanted to go to sleep.

***

In February 1962 my dear old godmother who lived in Hove had a stroke and was admitted to a nursing home. I hurried down to visit her and do what I could to comfort and reassure her. However, it was a very severe stroke, and two days later came the coup de grace, another massive stroke. Dudley and I attended to all the funeral arrangements and household affairs, telephoned those relations and friends in England and dispatched cables to those abroad. We also visited her solicitor and bank manager. Her affairs were in perfect order as one might well expect from someone long associated with and disciplined by the high standards of the diplomatic service.

As a consequence of her death, I inherited a legacy consisting of stocks and shares. My elder sister and brother also inherited a similar legacy, as she had been our aunt as well as my godmother. After the funeral ceremony and the sadness of her mortal death, my spirit revived and I began to look forward to the future once more. It occurred to me that if I realised the value of these stocks and shares, we would have enough capital to buy a little cottage of our own.

Dudley was now well established in the London office of Messrs Parry & Co of Madras. His much older brother had recently retired as chairman and managing director of the company in India and, following edicts issued by the Indian government of the time, an Indian had taken over. This vast British company, built up and maintained by hard-working Scots, Welsh and English people over the previous two hundred years, was now, following Indian independence, to be completely Indianised, and only a few British remained in their offices prior to their retirement. The new Indian chairman and managing director had personally assured Dudley that the London office would continue as it was and he would be employed there until his own retirement in 1980.

My godmother had always hoped we would eventually find ourselves a home of our own and her legacy would now make this possible. We decided to try and find a cottage in the Ditchling-Hassocks area, mainly because the commuter trains from Hassocks to Victoria Station in London were ideal for Dudley. We scanned all the local newspaper advertisements, but the price of most properties was far too high for us. We didn't give up the search, however, and continued making enquiries. Unfortunately, most of the properties within our price range were terraced houses in the towns, but our main interest was in a country cottage in an isolated position. Optimistically we just went on looking and hoping.

At the end of April 1963 Dudley fell ill and after various attempts to contain the trouble our doctor decided an operation was the only satisfactory solution. We were both rather anxious over the situation, so I suggested that a 'get well suit' might be a good stimulant and something Dudley could look forward to wearing when he was well again. Accordingly, we drove into

Lewes to visit a tailor in the High Street who had previously sold Dudley some very good shirts. When we arrived, Dudley asked to be shown some suiting materials, so the tailor's assistant ushered us into a workroom at the back of the shop where a large number of bolts of cloth in all sorts of shades and textures were neatly stacked on long shelves. There was also a large work-table and several chairs. A full-length cheval mirror dominated one side of the room and a big pile of pattern books lay invitingly on a small side table. Presently, the tailor joined us and after a careful inspection of various cloths and some discreet advice, Dudley chose the cloth he fancied as well as the style of suit that would complement his very long legs by having an extra long jacket with a light flare and single vent.

Next came the all-important ritual of the measurements. The tailor was a very tiny man and, in order to measure Dudley across the shoulders and around the chest, he asked his assistant to place a wooden, three-step mounting block directly behind Dudley's very upright figure. The tailor then mounted the block and, holding his tape measure firmly in his small hands, started the ritual by calling out the measurements to his assistant who wrote them down in a big leather-bound book. He then stepped down from the mounting block and the remaining measurements were done from floor level. All his movements were carried out with a ceremonial dignity and quiet assurance. His profound awareness of the importance of his ancient craft created a timeless atmosphere in which we could all play a part. It was traditional craftsmanship at its very best—an occasion to be remembered with real pleasure.

When everything was duly completed, with all the decisions on style and stitching agreed, we explained to the tailor about Dudley's coming operation and the reason for the new suit. He received this news with great understanding and much real sympathy. He suggested a date after the operation for the final fitting and, with many good wishes, escorted us to the door of his shop and said farewell.

Before Dudley was due to go into hospital, I asked him if he would like to try some of Dr Edward Bach's Flower Remedy essences to calm his thoughts and prepare him for the surgeon. He accepted at once and continued taking them after the operation as well. The operation duly took place in the Hayward's

Heath Cottage Hospital and was a complete success. Dudley's rapid recovery and low level of pain puzzled the surgeon and the anaesthetist. The day following the operation, the surgeon phoned me to report on Dudley's recovery. There was a puzzled note in his voice as he said, "I'm amazed that Mr Tod is not having much more pain. It was the largest prolapsed pile I have ever removed. Your husband is refusing sleeping pills and drugs, yet he's making the quickest recovery I've ever seen!" I expressed my delight at this and thanked him for his surgical skill. I could still detect a puzzled note in his voice so I told him that Dudley had been and still was taking Dr Bach Rescue Remedy, a wild flower essence. After a pause, this kind and dedicated man said, "Ah, well—whatever it is, your husband is making amazing progress and I'm very happy about it. It's quite—well, er—miraculous!" I knew enough about medical etiquette not to say any more.

Dudley came home in record time. He looked well and was very thankful that the operation had been so successful. He told me that the anaesthetist, when he came to visit him, had asked what he was taking to ease the pain. He was very anxious to know because he himself was due to have the operation and dreaded the thought of the pain. Dudley showed him the little bottle of Rescue Remedy, telling him it was a mixture of wild flower essences preserved in brandy, and that the dose was four drops in a little water to be taken frequently when the pain was severe. "Oh, is that all it is?" demanded the anaesthetist in a mocking sort of way. "It may sound simple," Dudley assured him, "but you have seen for yourself how well it has worked for me. I am sure it would help you too." "Oh, well, I don't really know, " said the anaesthetist doubtfully, fingering the small bottle and then replacing it on the bedside locker. "I just don't know . . . ." As he said this, Dudley realised that this highly trained medical man just could not accept that wild flowers were so powerful. There was simply nothing more to say.

Dudley's convalescence was a happy time for both of us, and soon the afternoon arrived for the final fitting of the 'get well suit'. We drove into Lewes full of excitement. The tailor greeted us and congratulated Dudley on the success of his operation. Then we went into the back room and the suit was brought in for the fitting. The tailor gave anxious little clicks with his tongue as he helped Dudley into the trousers. For the jacket, he insisted on mounting his little block and holding out the jacket for Dudley to slip his arms into, then climbing down moved around to the front to button it up. I gave a gasp of pleasure and clapped my hands. It looked marvellous! The little tailor turned and gave me a ceremonial bow from the waist. "What a perfect fit!" we all agreed, laughing happily together. Certainly, the 'get well suit' had created its own magic. Dudley really looked splendid and the tailor and his assistant glowed with pride; their craftsmanship was indeed worthy of praise.

Leaving the tailor's shop, we passed the rather posh local office of Strutt & Parker, Lofts & Warner, Estate Agents. In their display window, amongst photographs of large estates and various mansions, was one of a beautiful little stone cottage, obviously renovated extensively and standing in an exquisite and elaborately landscaped garden. Naturally, the price was enormous. I sighed as we gazed at it and said to Dudley, "I wonder if, by some miracle, they might have a cottage on their books that has not been expensively renovated that we could buy and make habitable at a reasonable cost." He smiled down at me, gave my arm a squeeze and in his gentle voice said, "Let's go in and enquire. They may be grand estate agents of vast properties but you never know unless you ask. They may even have a little place available belonging to one of their estates."

So we went into the beautifully carpeted office which was surrounded by dozens of large photographs of even larger houses. A quietly spoken, middle-aged woman behind the vast counter listened carefully to our requirements, hesitated for a few seconds and then said with a delightful smile, "The Danny Estate have a cottage available on long lease—it's condemned at the moment, but you might like to look at it." She slipped the particulars out of a file and handed them to us, again with a lovely smile. By this time, my heart was beating loudly and the excitement rising within me was explosive. I struggled to control it. Whatever happened I must keep calm!

Dudley thanked the kind woman and told her we would view the property the following day and telephone her our impressions, with a view to further negotiation if it proved suitable. She told us where we could locate the key to the cottage and, with the particulars firmly clutched in Dudley's hand, we left the office and dashed home. Once we were safely inside the living room of our converted potting shed, we read the details over with great care. The property, part of the Danny Estate, was called Warren Farm, but as no farm land was being leased with the property, the name was now to be changed to The Warren off New Way Lane, and the lease was to be for 99 years. There was no piped water, no electric light and no indoor sanitation. The purchaser would have to effect all the alterations and improvements to make it habitable, and there was the possibility of a local improvement grant. Above all, it was almost exactly what we had asked for and it was no wonder the woman had smiled when she produced the particulars.

It was quite an undertaking to buy and then restore a condemned cottage. It would involve an architect, a builder and a whole lot of common sense and self-discipline on our part, but it was a challenge which filled me with excitement. I would gladly sink my entire legacy into such a wonderful opportunity and, if it did prove to be the house Mrs Howard and I had seen two years before, it was something I must do! Dudley agreed that if it was possible we should go ahead and he too was fascinated by the idea of resurrecting a condemned cottage.

As I read and re-read the particulars, I became increasingly convinced that it *was* the small house up the long chalk track. But was it really? There were at least seven cottages in New Way Lane, and it wouldn't be until the following morning, when we had the key and instructions as to how to locate the cottage, that we could be quite certain. As we lay in bed that night, my excitement kept on bubbling up and I couldn't settle down. My instinct was so strong that it must be that magical place which had drawn me to itself so powerfully two years previously. At length, exhausted by so much excitement, I feel asleep.

The following day we drove to Danny House by the main road from Hassocks to Hurstpierpoint and were given the key and our instructions. The house, once a farmhouse, was the last one on the right hand side of New Way Lane leading down to the Matsfield Arms public house. It lay up a winding chalk track just above a big Sussex barn. So, it really *was* the little house Mrs Howard and I had seen two years before! My excitement knew no bounds. We drove along the lane to the foot of the chalk track, parked the car in a small lay-by and walked up the track.

The big Sussex barn was on our right and just above it the beech wood started climbing up the hillside, row upon row of large trees clustered close together. On the left was the little Tudor farmhouse, standing quite alone and empty. We opened the garden gate, walked up the path, inserted the key and opened the door. As we did so, the house welcomed us with little creaks and whispers. Eagerly we went inside and standing in the large living room we heard the wind sighing softly in the great inglenook fireplace. Outside, the sound of birdsong was tumultuous, then a cock pheasant gave a loud call and we stood rooted to the spot. The peace and serenity of the old house, the wild garden full of box hedges and marigolds and the surrounding beech and sycamore trees made ordinary conversation seem intrusive. We just stood, looked and listened and as I gazed out of the window a flight of bees went by. A blackbird perched in the cherry tree sang its beautiful melody and I knew we had been seen. The natural world was alert to our arrival and we were being observed.

A staircase in one corner of the living room led up to the three bedrooms above, and from that level another staircase went up to the second floor. In the bedroom above the living room I looked out of the window towards a large wood on the other side of the field below us. I then turned my eyes to the left and saw the top of the rise in the lane where I had stood two years before, looking back on this house with such a conviction within me. Now I was inside the house looking back to the very spot where I had stood. My spoken words had been answered and the promise made then was being fulfilled. This magical place was to be our home and from here I would slowly progress through the Maze and experience the real wonder and mystery of the natural world.

The house was indeed in an isolated situation on the lower slopes of Wolstanbury Hill with the landscape flowing all about it. It was so perfect I could hardly believe that all my wishes had been granted. I waited for the spell to break but it never did, nor ever has. Every weekday evening and at weekends Dudley was in his element, organising surveys, signing contracts, visiting architects and builders. He managed to obtain the maximum grant from the local council and arranged for piped water and electricity to be brought to the house.

I undertook to paint the inside walls, ceilings and doors, and to choose and arrange the furnishings, curtains and floor coverings, and we were both soon totally absorbed in our various tasks. We also found a builder from Hurstpierpoint—a quietly spoken Quaker and a dedicated craftsman—who had a great love for the Tudor period and understood their methods of building. He and his men renovated and repaired the house without changing its character in any way. They were obviously interested in its construction, as so little had been altered over the centuries.

As the work progressed, one of the shopkeepers in Hassocks asked me about it, saying, "How is the haunted house shaping up? Are you still sure you want to live there? I can't say that I'd care to!" His remarks surprised me and I asked him the reason for them. It appeared that hundreds of years earlier the farmer who lived there had been shot dead by smugglers carrying illicit wines and spirits from Brighton via Pyecombe to Danny and Hurstpierpoint. Apparently he had disturbed them unexpectedly and, wanting to arrest them, he hurried back to his house to get his gun. The smugglers realised his intention, pursued him and shot him just before he reached the house. One could easily imagine his terror and anguish as, mortally wounded, he desperately tried to avoid them and get inside to find his gun. The dramatic story of his violent death had remained vivid in the local folk history. I shuddered with sympathy towards the dead man as I heard the details. The shopkeeper insisted that over the years many local people claimed to have seen the ghost of the dead farmer dashing towards the house, and heard his cries of agony as he blundered about, unable to reach his gun. For this reason no one went up there after dark, and some, even to this day, were still very fearful. The shopkeeper ended his story in a very strange way by telling me the ghost's name was 'George'! "Just you look out for George!" were his parting words, uttered with a shrill note in his voice, as though the telling of the tale had revived old memories for him.

I was not afraid of George. I wanted to help this tormented soul to be released from the bondage of fear. It seemed best to wait until I was alone in the house, when the atmosphere would be undisturbed by the aura of others. I would hold him in the white light and suggest he followed this light and came out of the web of thought which held him to the place of his violent death, which had come about so suddenly and unexpectedly. After I had done this, all impressions of any such presence departed and the serenity of the house remained completely undisturbed. My earnest prayer had simply been that he would follow the Light, and find his way out of the dark web of thought into the reality of eternity.

By the end of April 1964 everything about the house was completed except for the electric light and power connection, which would be made in July or August. In the meantime we had a lamp, a candelabra holding five candles, a small calor gas stove and plenty of firewood all around us. Accordingly, we decided to move in and the removal van brought our belongings from the converted potting shed and deposited them in The Warren. It was a glorious day and all went well, but after six years in a croft the staircase in the house was quite a novelty. By the end of the first day my legs were aching from running up two flights of stairs and down again. We stayed up very late arranging furniture and unpacking crockery. The new curtains and the rush matting glowed in the lamplight as first twilight and then darkness fell. At last we were safe in our own home—the date was May 2nd, and it was a day to remember!

At 5 am the following morning we walked up the chalk path in our pyjamas. The great beech and sycamore trees waved their branches in the gentle breeze, and the early morning sunshine shafted through the leaves creating a dappled pathway of white and gold, mingling with the green of the downland above. I noticed agrimony, wild marjoram, plantain, dandelions and foxgloves growing on the banks, with a great clump of wild garlic momentarily scenting the air with its pungent odour. Primroses and violets, windflowers and dog's mercury carpeted the woodland glades. As we reached the top of the rise, the downland air was sweet and fresh, the fields on either side sparkled in the sunshine, and all was upspoilt and verdant. We were in the centre of the natural world, truly a paradise on earth.

This was a timeless place, full of natural magic. No wonder everyone wanted to share it with us: family, friends, members of the WSC and many others came to visit us, and many came to stay. The house always seemed to be filled with people from all corners of the Earth. Its fascination captured each one of them in turn—it really was such a magical place. But, inevitably, there were times when I felt so tired of cooking meals, making beds, cleaning and sweeping, or just doing all the usual domestic chores within the house. It was always better out of doors, collecting firewood and herbs. The elemental energies revived me. The question-and-answer sessions, of which I was doing a great many, also helped. The absent healing group members, who now came to The Warren regularly, were an even more wonderful stimulant. We all felt the benefit of these meetings. 'As you give, so you receive'—how true these words are.

My awareness gently urged me on, overcoming my anxiety and puzzlement as to the task to be done. Was it to be done here or was it here I would learn and understand the final instructions? The sheer perfection of the place and its surroundings satisfied my every need. Our coming here had been so beautifully arranged for us; was it perhaps a 'gift of love' to prepare me for the task which would take me away from this paradise? These thoughts filled me with apprehension, and then suddenly I found myself reciting William Blake's poem 'Eternity', over and over again. It was the poem Gerald Bullett had taught me, and it was as if his spirit was reassuring me, making me feel that 'He who kisses the joy as it flies, Lives in eternity's sunrise'. Here I was, in a perfect centre of the natural world, and in nature everything has a meaning. I would indeed 'kiss the joy as it flies'. These words were like a balm to my troubled thoughts—they made me realise the answer would come in its own good time, and that I must keep alert and positive, ready for anything.

The spring, summer, autumn and winter of our first year at The Warren was a wonderful time of discovery on all levels. To our delighted surprise, we found we were sharing the house with birds, bats and bees. The birds nested under the eaves, keeping up a constant chatter, especially when the fledglings began to fly. They were mostly noisy starlings, dressed in their glittering feathers and using their mimic voices to create confusion and amusement. The bees made their comb under the overhanging tiles on the front of the house; sometimes traces of excess honey dribbled down from above. I wondered if these were the same bees we had seen on our first visit, as they 'flighted' past the living room window. Now, at least, we knew where they lived! The bats were much more elusive. I first saw them at twilight, zooming out from under the top tiles above a bedroom window. They seemed to flash out like arrows from a bow, in perfect formation, their inbuilt radar enabling them to exit and re-enter the space under the tiles without any error. They were the tiny pipistrelle variety, and once a mother bat, with her baby clinging to her back, came into the kitchen. I caught both her and the clinging baby in my hands and gently released them outside again, close to their home under the tiles. The pair were so tiny, they easily fitted into the palms of my hands, and they were soft and quiet like little mice whilst I held them. I peered at the mother's face—it resembled exactly one of the medieval gargoyles at Clayton Parish Church. Were they perhaps the models for some medieval stonecarver's craft?

At the end of the year, on December 30th, Dr Alice Gilbert came to stay and see in the New Year of 1965 with us. With her luggage came a load of files and boxes, which rather surprised me until I learned that she had brought them along in the hope that I would take over her job of Hon. Sec. of the World Spiritual Council. How extraordinary, I thought—and why me of all people? I listened to her, though, and then thought about it carefully. Could this be part of the task? Was this why we were here? The Warren was not a very suitable place for making quick contacts and attending meetings in Tunbridge Wells and London. I thought again, closed my eyes and waited, until a clear 'no' came through, which confirmed my own instinct. I would have to be more than diplomatic, though, in my choice of words to convey to Alice that I could not accept the honour she had offered me. Since our move to The Warren I was becoming increasingly sure that the task lay in and with the natural world, and not in towns or buildings, or amongst a large number of people interested in conferences and committees. In my own mind I felt certain that the task had to be done out of doors, in the open countryside. Unfortunately, Alice took my carefully worded refusal rather badly, but eventually accepted my decision, and we turned the conversation harmoniously onto other subjects.

I was still very interested to know more about the previous occupants of The Warren, and particularly its history in connection with the Danny Estate over more than four hundred years.

Alice became interested too and suggested her friend, the well known and respected trance medium, Mrs Dorothy Robins, who lived near Brighton, should come and hold a 'sitting' in the living room and I could ask questions about the house, the previous occupants and their way of life. All was duly arranged by telephone, and on Saturday January 2nd 1965 Dudley drove Alice over the downs to fetch Mrs Robins. Meanwhile I stayed behind to tidy up the living room and prepare a tea of sandwiches and cakes which we would take together when the sitting was over. The thought of meeting Mrs Robins excited me and the prospect of hearing about the old house and its previous occupants added to this. Already questions were forming in my mind. I knew that Mrs Robins was a very reliable medium who had helped many famous people with accurate information, and I felt sure I would learn a great deal about the house with her help. How very fortunate I was.

Dorothy Robins was a delightful person, warm and friendly, with soft dark eyes and curly grey hair. There was an aura of quiet dignity about her. I felt confident and happy as we settled down to start the sitting. Alice offered to write the words down as Dorothy delivered them, keeping a complete record of the event. After a quiet period and a prayer of protection, Dorothy asked me to give her a very personal object of mine to hold, something only I had worn. I gave her my little signet ring which had been made for me in India, and which only I had worn. I then waited expectantly for the sitting to start so that I could ask my questions about the house and its history. However, to my complete amazement, words came gushing out so quickly from Mrs Robins that Alice had difficulty in keeping up with them. Firstly, there was a long and detailed message of information about the task, with layer after layer being revealed to me. All the information was given with infinite patience and care—I just listened and listened, responding occasionally. There were also many personal messages concerning other aspects of my life, and I did learn a great deal about The Warren and its past history.

These are some of the relevant phrases from the long message which Alice wrote down for me, as Dorothy, deep in a trance, spoke them out aloud:

"You have played many parts (experienced many incarnations). You are philosophical and have the ability to study and absorb knowledge. A writer you knew named Gerald Bullett is close to you; concentrate on him. He can help you with your choice of words, their meaning, sense and impact. He was a philosopher in Greece in a previous incarnation. You were also in Greece. This life arches over to that one. In this life you have to finish something started then. Your helpers are in the past. The information you receive is from ancient Greece but brought up to date. Music, singing, dancing—words and actions—your whole body is attuned. Spirit has been waiting. There is in you a completeness. Within yourself you have the ability to be complete without child or lover. Spread *in* not *out* is best for you. You might think 'I yearn' but in reality you do not. You can be satisfied. Out of the body are those who enter in and understand. You can be complete in yourself as you work and write. The Master wants you to know this because it answers so many of your questions, this complete circle of yourself. But you must still go out to other people, more and more. There is a reason for your life. You have scope. Use it!

"The strongest influence in your present life is Grecian. There is a 'litany' of words and actions which you must bring out and write down. If not, you are living for your own delight. Pan comes with you out of trees, leaves, flowers, plants, sun and moon—lots of draperies 'hooked' to the stars, etc. As best as you can, give it to others, otherwise you will pass out of the body and the world will be the loser. The more you give, the more you will get. Sculpture, arches, pillars of thought. Very extraordinary—but you *had* to be told. You are surrounded by light and colour. Out of the body you are with the Group—you in, they out—they can give through you and so can finish their unfinished work which is simple yet profound. Please try to write it; do not go out of the body without having *tried* to complete this task. You have been given shape, forms, designs. Deepest truths are often defined by shape."

Q: Which is your favourite wild flower?
A: The buttercup.

"You are not a buttercup like your favourite wild flower. You are a big golden flower of wisdom and cosmic consciousness. Remember this, it is an important symbol. In ancient Greece you were the speaker and leader of the Group which travelled far and wide working with the natural forces. The final part of the Group's work was not finished. Now, in this incarnation you, as speaker and leader, must arrange for the work to be completed. This time you must also be the scribe (the completion of the work must be recorded—written down). Those members of the Group who are not of the body will cooperate with you, as we mentioned previously.

"You have a new slice of your life to come. You have to go somewhere you have not yet been to in this incarnation. This talking has been for your enlightenment. Too often you have hidden your light under a bushel. Now it must come out! Your husband, Dudley, will help you. He has promised to do so, with love and in gratitude for the help which you gave him in a previous incarnation—as you give so you receive."

When the sitting ended, we remained together in silence. The atmosphere surrounding us was cool and fragrant. The sensation was magical, and reluctantly we slowly opened our eyes and smiled at one another with perfect contentment. The unity had been complete and powerful. I expressed my thanks to Mrs Robins and the Teacher for all they had revealed to me, and to Alice Gilbert for having written it all down. I also felt great relief that, at last, I had been told about the task—although not yet how or where it was to be performed. That would surely come later. With the Teacher's help I would now be able to receive further information if I worked carefully and used my pen in a positive and cooperative way. With faith and love we could all work together to finish the unfinished work. I was now quite certain that the necessary information would be given to me if I kept detached but alert and willing to act. Saturday January 2nd 1965 was indeed one of the most important days in my life.

For several days after the sitting I pondered on the amazing quality of Mrs Robins's work. To bring through so much accurate information and so much love and comfort to so many different people and not to know what was said, unless the sitter told her afterwards or showed her the written words, was to me quite extraordinary. During the sitting I had been aware of her calm strength which came, I was now quite sure, from her complete trust and faith in the Creator of all life. Her work was totally selfless, putting no pressure on those asking the questions or those answering them. It was not until late in her life that grateful sitters brought their new-fangled tape recorders to the sittings and played them over to her afterwards. Then, and only then, did she hear her own voice talking, and have her own acts of faith revealed to her.

I also pondered over the messages which Mrs Robins had given me with the help of the Teacher. It had all come so unexpectedly. I had been looking forward to receiving information about the house and its previous occupants! It was so typical of my Group's wisdom to tell me, to remind me, of something so important when I was least expecting it. Here was the message, given to me without my asking, for which I had been waiting so long. The impact was profound. My awareness of Greece was only faint in my present consciousness, but this message started to revive ancient memories and, now as I understood it better, an ancient promise. My love of wild flowers and herbs, my yearning for the simple, pastoral life, close to the natural world and its inhabitants, my love of landscape and clear light: all these veiled sensations and longings were now revealed to me as being closely related to my past life in ancient Greece. It was like a joyful homecoming, and made sense of so much that had puzzled me. It also sharpened my cosmic consciousness and opened up a channel through which further information could come. But above all it taught me the *real* value of waiting patiently for the right moment.

***

Daily life at The Warren continued on its active way. People came and went. Small children, visiting with their parents, became enchanted by the house, the gardens and the surrounding woods. One little girl of four flatly refused to leave when the time came to return home to Tunbridge Wells. Her face flushed with determination as she said, "I'm staying here. This is a magic place; it's fairyland." She came and stood by me, holding fast to my hand. I knew exactly how she felt but the expression on her parents' faces distressed me, so I said, "Yes it is fairyland;

come with me to pick a magic rose to take with you, and with it you will take part of fairyland home with you." We picked the flower carefully so as not to be pricked by a thorn, and with constant stops to glance back her parents gradually persuaded her to get into their waiting car. With the flower firmly clutched in her small hand, she waved a tearful goodbye. How well I recalled the agony of leaving such a magical place when I was her age.

On every fine day, the dog and I went for downland walks and collected firewood in the copse. Sometimes the cats came too—they loved dashing through the woods, hiding and jumping into trees like minute tigers in the jungle. In spring and summer we found early purple orchids growing in clumps around the edge of the fields, and pyramid, bee and butterfly orchids grew in our wild garden. In one field above us we found thousands of cowslips nodding their heads in the wind, and their scent filled the air when the sun was bright. We loved to sit among them inhaling their sweetness and listening to the larks singing overhead. Richard Jeffries, the naturalist, was right: "Wolstanbury Hill," he wrote, "has a Grecian air about it." This recognition delighted me. With what infinite care the Group had chosen The Warren for us!

Pheasants belonging to the Danny Estate visited us regularly. One morning as I was standing by an upstairs window, I witnessed a beautiful sight: a superb cock pheasant, his brilliantly coloured plumage iridescent in the sunlight, slowly paraded in courtly fashion side by side with his demure little hen in her dappled plumage along the length of the long path beneath the rose pergola. They hesitated now and then to peck at some morsel on the ground and then communicate with one another by excited little chirps before moving on. How splendid they seemed in their natural state when undisturbed by human beings. Their charm and elegant beauty were a joy to behold.

On another occasion we were just finishing breakfast when we saw a young fox creeping across the lawn outside the dining room window, which ran from floor to ceiling. He was moving with great caution, keeping close to the ground. His prey was the cluster of fat we had recently put out for the birds, and with infinite care he captured it and devoured it quickly. In doing so, however, he came closer to the window and saw his own reflection in the bottom pane of glass. The expression on his face was marvellous to see: in quick succession came surprise, curiosity, puzzlement and alarm; then with a furious yelp he sprang towards his own reflection and landed against the window with a loud bump. He recovered quickly, shook himself and with but one backward glance fled into the woods.

High above our wood-shed door, in their little dovecote, lived Serena and Sebastian, our two white doves, a gift from Evelyn Peat of Ditchling. The sound of their deep-throated cooing created a peaceful and romantic atmosphere at that end of the house. On fine days they liked to strut about on the high roof of The Warren viewing the surrounding landscape and the activities of the other birds. At dusk they would circle the house several times in a high flight before coming in to roost in their own little dovecote and enjoy their exotic foods such as Persian hemp, which was their real favourite. At their end of the house a number of sumac trees grew into exquisite shapes, their green foliage turning into liquid fire in the autumn. Doves and sumac trees from Arabia blended delicately into the soft downland setting.

After a while, we began to notice that the rooms in the house were steadily filling up with books. So many friends and visitors brought us copies of their favourite authors, and authors brought us copies of their latest publications. They all seemed to know about our love of books and we were so grateful to them for their warm-hearted generosity. Fortunately, Dudley was very good at making bookshelves! On our various walls we had oil and water-colour paintings by our friends Margaret Forbes, Rhoda Waley, A Jennings and Sidney Colverson. We also hung a few of my own designs and wild flower paintings. Our largest picture was a beautiful oil painting of my father in naval uniform, wearing his decorations. It had been painted by his old friend James Barraclough, a professional portrait painter much in vogue in the 1920s and '30s. I loved walking around the house looking at the pictures and the shelves of books. They were such a beautiful reflection of our many friends. Our home was indeed a house of gifts.

Days, weeks, months slipped by leaving indelible memories of encounters with unusual and fascinating people, of conversations quite out of this world and meditations shared in the silence, of walks on the open downland and in the woods, surrounded by the wonder and magic of the natural world. However, our second year at The Warren ended in a most dramatic way. One evening in mid-December Dudley returned home looking exhausted and very pale. I was alarmed and urged him to sit by the Inglenook fireplace and warm up whilst I fetched him a stiff whisky. I sat down beside him wondering what on earth had happened to make him appear so distressed. After a while he said simply, "I have been made redundant. The Indian government will not allow enough money to be transferred from Madras to pay all the staff in the London office. My job will cease to exist after March of next year, 1966."

I was appalled by this sudden news, a complete reversal of what Dudley had been told only three months previously by the chairman and managing director of the company when he had visited London and assured Dudley that his job would be secure until his retirement. This latest news made me realise how frail and fallible are the words of a human being when national and financial winds of change start to blow. Parry's—a vast British company with huge factories producing sugar, pottery, fertilisers, alcohol and sweets, with branches all over India—had been carefully built up by employing a small number of British subjects and thousands of Indians in all their factories and offices. This company, in which Dudley's grandfather and elder brother had played such an important part and to which Dudley himself had devoted so many years of his life, was now completely Indianised and, because of the Indian government's restriction on the transfer of money, his redundancy payment was very small indeed. It was a terrible shock but together we found the way to adjust and start again. For the next three years, Dudley attended interviews and obtained a number of temporary jobs, but nothing permanent materialised.

Gradually I became aware that our time at The Warren was coming to an end. The next and final move to the place where the task would be completed would happen when the time was right. In spite of my physical distress and heartache at the thought of leaving our home, I knew if I asked questions in the right way the Group would give me correct answers, because it was Group work which had to be completed. I had absolute faith in their integrity and their wisdom. It was just the waiting, the time element, which was so difficult and, once again,

William Blake's short poem 'Eternity'—the poem Gerald Bullett had taught me—helped to balance my fluttering emotions. I would not be overcome if I kept faith with the words and their meaning, which was so important. Complete awareness of detachment in its most positive aspect—love—and also the helpful and supportive message about Dudley, which came at the end of the long sitting with Dorothy Robins at the beginning of 1965, made it abundantly clear that the task I had undertaken would finally be completed with Dudley's help and support. How complex and delicate are these spiritual links and what good sense they made of life's apparent difficulties. My recognition of Dudley when we met in Cambridge had been hazy and vague but my intuition, my eternal memory, had been true and exact, overcoming outward confusion and showing the way. The message of January 2nd 1965 confirmed this and made a pattern I could follow if I kept alert and aware of the Group's instructions. Once again I was reminded of those powerful words: 'God helps those who help themselves.'

***

In 1967 Dudley decided that he would join the Rosicrucian Order which had a meeting place in Brighton. He asked me to join too, but I knew that this was something he had to do on his own, using his own awareness and developing his talents in mathematics and physics. I also realised his military training in disciplined reconnaissance and careful strategy, learned and perfected over many centuries, was going to be of vital importance to us over the next few years. He attended the Rosicrucian meetings and meditations regularly and made some good friendships with several members, interesting people from all walks of life. Five of them became our close friends and have remained so. The well-known water-colour artist SR Badmin (Roy to us all) and his wife, Rosaline, were particularly kind to us, and their young daughter, Galea, radiant in her youth and love of life, brought us much joy. Margaret Atkinson, a retired Foreign Office official who had been one of the first women vice-consuls in Germany after the 1939-45 war came to The Warren to have question-and-answer sessions with me. Joan Page-Henderson, another member, was a marvellous character who had completely overcome adversity with a wickedly humorous tongue, much self-discipline and a philosophical acceptance of her life. She was a true musician who played the piano with infinite skill and a profound awareness of the healing power of music.

Great pleasure and much joy flowed between us all. I found that the company of these stimulating people, our many friends in the WSC, the healing groups which I still ran and the question-and-answer script work undertaken in the beautiful surroundings of The Warren all helped me to overcome feelings of sadness at leaving the area. Also, like a bright and comforting light was my belief that the Group would direct us to another magical house, also in beautiful surroundings, where the task would be completed. It would not be easy—we would have to make a great effort—but the reward would be tremendous. To my great joy, I discovered that working in close communion with the Group and the knowledge that we are not alone on this planet, or anywhere else, acted as a spur.

The month of March 1968 was a very active one for both of us. Kay Poulton, who visited us regularly for question-and-answer sessions, meals and conversation, had become very interested in the Radionic Association, which had its centre at Burford in Oxfordshire. They were holding their annual weekend conference at the Queen's Hotel in Hastings, Sussex. Kay was eager for me to accompany her and to learn about their healing techniques and, since I have always been interested in healing methods, I agreed to go.

We travelled by train from Brighton to Hastings and took a taxi to the hotel. A large number of members filled the place, but everything was most efficiently organised, very sophisticated and friendly. The energy being created was very strong and soon after we arrived I saw two people I immediately knew I had to meet. At first I thought they were twins—they were so close—then I discovered they were man and wife. Their names were Cecil and Evelyn Heathfield and both were artists who lived in a studio in Lewes. Cecil was tall, thin and gentle, constantly looking at all around him, taking in every detail as trained artists do. Evelyn, who had a gently rounded form, also watched, her eyes sparkling and alert. They both had a bubbling sense of humour which caused them to laugh and talk together in a compelling way. To my delight they came and sat next to me and drew me into their conversation. It was just like meeting old friends—words flowed so easily, cascading into laughter and a quick recognition of one another. During the weekend, between lectures and demonstrations, we spent exhilarating hours together talking and listening. Their love of the arts was complete and totally absorbing. Together they had brought into being the Lewes Little Theatre, an amazing achievement involving years of hard work and dedication. Cecil had long been a governor of the Sussex Rural Musical Society, holding it all together in a masterly way, encouraging musicians to perform and audiences to appreciate good music. He had also been a prison visitor for many years giving help and true compassion where it was most needed.

My immediate interest in these two people rather surprised me at first, but the reason was soon revealed to me: we were members of the same cosmic Group, meeting again for a particular reason. Within days of my return to The Warren, I received a letter from Evelyn Heathfield inviting me to visit them in their Lewes studio which lay below the castle ramparts in Paddock Lane. It had once been a big storage barn used by carriers who brought agricultural products into the city from the surrounding countryside, and here they stored their produce in the upper part of the building while housing their horses and carts in the stables and sheds below. When this type of trading ceased, the building gradually fell into a state of decay and neglect, as so often happens when fashions and trades alter. Evelyn had discovered it one day standing empty and forlorn, with a very large 'For Sale' sign on it which jutted out into the lane like a beacon.

A few days prior to this discovery Cecil had suddenly said to her: "What we need is a big barn which we can convert into a studio." To find something like this was no easy task in an old city like Lewes, but Evelyn's footsteps had been guided into Paddock Lane, where the property stood complete with its 'For Sale' sign. This immediate response to Cecil's request startled and then delighted them both. Without delay they bought it and had the upper barn converted into a large studio with a kitchen and bathroom off it, and one bedroom. The stables and cartsheds were then transformed into a superb exhibition room to hold paintings and sculpture. It became a centre for many other crafts too, like woodwork and pottery. A French window off the studio gave direct access to a large garden which climbed steeply upwards to ancient trees and the castle walls. In one corner, close to the walls, were the remains of a hermitage which seemed to emanate gentle and infinitely harmonious vibrations. A sweet stillness surrounded it which drew people in need of peace and quiet to sit there and meditate.

The windows on the opposite side of the studio looked down into the lane, and beyond across school playing fields to Mount Harly in the distance. The contrast was quite fascinating. At one end of the studio, completely covering the top half of the wall, Evelyn had painted a mural giving the impression of a huge window looking onto a rural scene in the Snowdonia National Park—an area they both dearly loved and had, over many years, visited frequently for painting and hill climbing. They both had a passion for rocks and stones, as well as small pieces of wood weathered to a delicate silver shade by wind and rain. They brought many of these beautiful objects home, where Cecil drew them and made etchings from them, each minute detail carefully and lovingly recorded. In turn, from these he created exquisite pictures in shape and form—each a miracle of line and texture.

During his working life Cecil had been a professional graphic artist with his own studios in London, travelling up each day from Lewes by train. Evelyn, who had lived all her life in Lewes where her father had been a doctor, was a qualified landscape designer and gardener (who just wanted to paint). She also became, in later life, a trained Cabbalist. As part of her training as a landscape gardener she had attended a horticultural college where she met and became friends with Violet Firth who later became well-known as Dion Fortune, author of many occult books and the founder of the Society of the Inner Light. Her amazing life story has already been well documented and most of her books are still in print. Evelyn and Violet never met again during their lifetimes, but because of their common interest in the Cabbala, a link was eventually made, after Violet's death, through question-and-answer sessions with me and my pen.

After my first visit to the Lewes studio Evelyn suggested I came again for a question-and-answer session as she had so many questions to ask. At first I hesitated: I had never done transposed writing in someone else's home. I was apprehensive about the atmosphere and sounds of the city and the ancient castle. But I did go, and all was well. Dion Fortune (Violet Firth) came through strongly and the two old friends had a fascinating reunion. Comments and queries flew across the pages. It was the start of a long and interesting correspondence between them, via my pen, which lasted until Evelyn's death in 1980 at the age of 86. Many other friends and members of Evelyn's family also wrote messages. Olive Pixley, founder of the Armour of Light (of which Evelyn had been a founder member) made eager contact and again the two friends had a long and interesting correspondence. Thus, the meeting at the Hastings Radionic Conference had indeed been for a particular reason.

Dudley's busy time in March 1968 came when he attended his first Rosicrucian weekend conclave at the Ship Hotel in Brighton. I joined him for the dinner and dance. It was a very happy occasion and we met a large number of members from other groups up and down the country. All had distinctive personalities linked by a common interest in the Rosicrucian Order and its teachings. These ancient orders have a subtle and detached way of linking their members through tradition, dignity and courtesy, enabling each person to respond to another with warmth and sincerity. It lifted my heart to see how Dudley was stimulated and helped by the Brighton Group meetings. New doors were opened which enabled him to use his knowledge of physics in a metaphysical way. His training in economics and business methods were being linked with spiritual aspects which he found interesting and revealing. His strong military connection was also being exercised in new and exciting ways. Likewise, his personal horizon was expanding greatly and the adventure of helping me to complete my task, spoken of by the Teacher in the message which came through Dorothy Robins in January 1965, was beginning to take shape.

As the years progressed, we both realised the time was fast approaching when we had to leave The Warren and move on. The vital message I had received from the Group, through Dorothy Robins, rested in my consciousness. It was information I had waited so long to receive. Now I knew I was preparing myself and slowly loosening my ties with The Warren. Dudley too was accepting the fact that no regular job would become available in the area. His determination had been wonderful to watch, but we were now united in our resolve to finish the work which I had started in ancient Greece and which must be completed, so that members of the Group could progress to new evolutionary activities. The responsibility was mine and I would discharge it with Dudley's cooperation. I would put our questions to the Group through the Teacher when we had made our final decisions, because I knew that the decisions had to be ours alone without influence from any quarter. This awareness of self-discipline and responsibility for one's actions was paramount.

I was confident that when we had made our clear and final decision we would receive help and guidance as and when it was needed and when it was right to ask for it. Meanwhile, the summer and the autumn days at The Warren were beautiful, and the longing to stay in this magical place was very strong. Such expressions as 'If only we could . . . . Wouldn't it be possible to . . . . ?' were often voiced by both of us. Our clear and final decision was going to be very difficult to make, in spite of all our resolve. We went for long walks through the woods and over the downland, 'remembering' the landscape, taking mental photographs to be safely stored away in our subconscious and then brought out and lingered over in the years to come, just like any conventional family album. In late autumn, as I walked through the woods, words like a well-remembered jingle kept on passing through my mind. The words were: "It's always best out of doors. Follow the ways of wild nature and find the Hill of Wisdom." The very words seemed to reflect the shapes and forms all around me and thinking on them brought me a sensation of eager anticipation, tempered by awe and wonder. They made me conscious of the closeness of Pan and that the task was directly connected with earth, air, fire, water and cosmic energy (the power of the Sun's rays).

I realised that these were just hints and reminders, but of what and where? I continually re-read the message received in January 1965, searching for further clues. It seemed to me the situation was so delicate and so vitally important I must not make a mistake now or assume too much. Faith and humility must be my watchwords. So often at times the Maze seemed more like a labyrinth, but I never lost sight of the Light or my awareness of the Golden Thread.

By the end of the year we had made our final and clear decision to sell The Warren. It was an irrevocable step which took much courage. It drew us very close together and reconfirmed our resolve. It was also a tremendous relief, which left the future wide open. We would have to make a completely fresh start.

1969 was indeed a year of revelation: the various strands of the Golden Thread were being drawn together to create a cord strong enough to support all that had to take place in such a short time. Our first piece of good fortune came when the government's Leasehold Reform Act finally became law. This enabled us to purchase our leasehold from the Danny Estate at a very modest price, and thereby we could put The Warren on the market as a freehold property and at a freehold price. Having decided to sell, the next decision concerned where we could move to and what job Dudley could find. We were in a position to go anywhere and to do anything. As we discussed the possibilities Dudley, in a gentle but firm way, said, "I want to be in an area where there is a Rosicrucian group." I agreed, because I realised this was part of the pattern we must follow.

Dudley fetched the list of Rosicrucian groups and started to read them out to me—Birmingham, Derby, Nottingham, Sheffield, London—they all sounded far too industrial. Then he read the name of Tiverton. Tiverton was in rural Devon and the name shone like a beacon! We hugged each other in delight and relief. Out came the maps; we put them flat on the floor as we searched for Tiverton. There it was—in North Devon, close to the west Somerset border. It stood out on the map, and we excitedly noted that it was surrounded by deep green countryside, moors and hills. Was this the 'somewhere I had not been to yet'? Could this be where I was to follow the ways of wild nature and find the Hill of Wisdom? All the rivers in the area seemed long, winding and, in places, wide and deep. It was an area neither of us knew, but something about it looked welcoming.

I spent days studying the area around Tiverton in detail on the map, looking at its shape and noting the contours, and each time I did so I felt a sense of keen anticipation, and an excited conviction started to grow inside me. Our decisions were consolidating—we were thinking things out. Presently, the time for asking questions would come.

On the 9th of February Dudley went to Brighton to attend a

meeting of all the English Rosicrucian Masters to discuss some important aspects and decisions regarding the Order's future. At this event Dudley met the Tiverton Master and learned that their meetings were held at Cove, a small village northeast of Tiverton, and not far from Bampton and the Somerset boundary. Dudley expressed a wish to come and live in the Tiverton area when we had sold our Sussex home. He was warmly welcomed and a visit to the area, to meet members and look at likely properties, was fixed for the middle of March. We both instinctively felt that this encounter in Brighton was a clear confirmation that our decision to move to the West Country was the right one.

On March 7th I joined the Heathfields at the annual weekend radionic conference in the Queen's Hotel in Hastings. It was a joyful occasion with much discussion, many interesting talks and healing demonstrations. The sound of laughter ringing within the lecture hall was a happy reminder of the healing power it contains; its actual benefit to the physical body is so often forgotten. A good loud laugh stimulates the liver, kidneys, heart and lungs. It is also a real breath of fresh air for the spirit.

During this weekend the Heathfields arranged to have a session in their bedroom with Armyn Wodehouse and her friend Lizzie McClaine. They asked me to come too, and Kay Poulton also joined us. The session was recorded on tape. Armyn was the speaker and told us many things concerning healing work already done, and about the work still to be undertaken. I recognised that a lot of what she was saying was similar to Dorothy Robins's instructions to me. Armyn named me as a leader of a Group working with the solar ray (so here was another confirmation). It was made clear that the work was with the soil and all its elements. It also confirmed that the Heathfields and myself belonged to the same Group. Armyn Wodehouse was well-known in esoteric circles—she was a member of the White Eagle Lodge, an active worker in the Radionic Association and had recently visited the Findhorn Community, having been drawn to them through their work with the nature spirits and the elemental kingdom.

I too had been carefully following the progress of Peter Caddy and his wife Eileen, together with their friends Dorothy Maclean and Robert Ogilvie Crombie, as they created the Findhorn Garden Community, which gradually evolved into the Findhorn

Foundation, now world famous. Ever since I had first heard about them from Clare Cameron and Sir George Trevelyan, I had felt a strong link with these folk. I have never met any of them, neither have I been able to visit the Foundation, but the link has remained powerful, positive and sure.

My strongest link has been with Robert Ogilvie Crombie through his work with the pure spirit of nature, who is Pan, and all the elementals. Roc (as he is usually known) was a scientist and a seer—a rare combination in the 20th century–and also a musician and a psychologist. His awareness of the life of trees and plants and their helpers in the elemental kingdom was similar to mine. His love of the natural world was boundless; he was also extremely conscious of how easily *homo sapiens* can exploit and exterminate the natural world and its myriad inhabitants by thoughtless greed and desire for power and prestige. Like the poet Gerard Manley Hopkins, he understood the value of the wilderness and how it can help to balance the frenetic and foolish activities of humans. Since Roc's death in 1975 I have received many messages from him, giving me information and awareness extremely helpful to me. It is he who has encouraged me to write these 'glimpses', as he calls them, so that others may know about the work, how it came about, and what it is 'in relation to the cosmos'.

On Sunday March 17th Dudley drove down to Devon to spend six days in the Tiverton area, meeting members of the Cove group and attending one of their meetings. He also contacted a number of estate agents and actually viewed several properties they had on offer, but none seemed suitable. The agents, however, were most anxious to help and promised to keep us advised by post and by telephone when further properties came onto their books. These six days in the West Country also gave Dudley time to drive around and explore the area. Moreover, it gave him valuable contacts with his fellow Rosicrucians. I instinctively felt it was important he should do this on his own, and feel quite free to make decisions regarding his future and ultimately the possibility of a job. He telephoned me regularly to say how much he was enjoying meeting the various members and that their Cove village meeting had been very rewarding as well as interesting—all good omens indeed.

Whilst Dudley was away, I once again studied the map of

North Devon and West Somerset with great care and concentration. As I searched over the area, my eyes were drawn to the name Wiveliscombe, a small market town on the Somerset and Devon border. The attraction was powerful. I focused in turn on Tiverton, Exeter, Bampton, deliberately creating a detached attitude, but my eyes kept on returning to Wiveliscombe. Why? Then, quite clearly, just above Wiveliscombe, I saw the name Huish Champflower. A tingling sensation went right along my arm as I put my index finger onto the name on the map. Huish Champflower! I spoke it aloud, and the sound seemed to resonate around me. What a strange and beautiful name it was—it sounded remote and ancient, like somewhere in a fairy tale. As I sat there contemplating it, my senses relaxed and a feeling of warmth and serenity surrounded me. I do not know how long I remained just staring at the map, my index finger resting on the name Huish Champflower. It was a timeless period of pure delight and enchantment.

After a while I started tracing over the surrounding area with my finger. The colour on the map was green, some darker, some lighter, indicating deep countryside. I then noticed that Huish Champflower lay on the edge of the Brendon Hills, a largely uninhabited area between Exmoor and the Quantock Hills. I found myself visualising Huish Champflower as a green and remote place, withdrawn from the 20th century and still retaining its ancient and hidden ways. Its name, half Anglo-Saxon, half Norman French, which could be interpreted as a household in a field of flowers, created a picture of ancient buildings surrounded by fragrant fields of herbs, grasses and wild flowers.

As I folded up the map, a direct conviction seemed to enter my being: a pattern was beginning to take shape, and I felt sure we had made the right decision to move to the West Country.

On Friday March 28th the annual Rosicrucian weekend conclave was due to be held in the Metropole Hotel, Brighton. Dudley had been appointed chairman and organiser some months previously, and in consequence he had been busy arranging the programme, contacting members and finalising arrangements with the hotel manager, making sure of a suitable menu and a lively dance band for the dinner and dance on the Saturday evening. As the 1969 chairman of the conclave, Dudley made the opening speech of welcome to all the dignitaries and members of the Order. Afterwards, members commented on what a wise, penetrating and humorous speech it had been, delivered with gentle wit and a well-modulated voice. I pondered deeply on this small miracle. I recalled the quite appalling stammer Dudley had when we first met at Cambridge University, and I knew the courage it had taken to stand up in front of a large number of people, all eagerly waiting to hear him *speak*! It was a great achievement and we both felt justifiably proud at the ovation he had received.

Once again, we thoroughly enjoyed the dinner, the dancing and the varied company of Masters and members. They were such a diverse collection of souls, but all had one interest in common—the Rosicrucian Order. Now that Dudley's visit to Tiverton and Cove had been accomplished, and the conclave in Brighton was successfully behind him, I felt it was about the right time to contact the Group through the Teacher and ask for their comments on our decision to move to the West Country. On Wednesday April 2nd, therefore, the time of the full moon, we had a question-and-answer session. After a period of quiet and prayers of protection the writing began. The Teacher, acting as spokesman, cordially greeted us both by name, and started the message as follows:

"We greet you.

We are aware of your need for reassurance. We come to help you. Your decision to sell The Warren was a very difficult one to come to, was it not?"

We both said, "Yes, it was."

The Teacher continued: "It was *right*, although on an earthly level it appears cruel to both of you. It is necessary to progress the Path of Light. You will be well helped on the physical level, so do not be troubled.

This move has to come about otherwise the solar work cannot progress. We need you in the right place for the completion of the solar work. We will be close to you as you work. Do not fear on the material level; that will be looked after as needed.

We will protect and guide you if you will trust us. Do you understand?"

We both said, "Yes, we do understand."

Dudley then said: "As I wish to continue my work and study

with the Rosicrucian Order, we plan to move into the Tiverton area where there is a group at Cove. Comments please."

The Teacher replied: "Yes, indeed, that is as we would wish. You will be in the right area for the solar work. In this area is much old wisdom which needs to be reactivated by those who are aware, as you both are. The ground is full of vibrations which need to be correctly activated to help humanity to lift itself up.

We will direct you to the right area in which to look for a dwelling. Study the contours on the map. Use your highest concentration. Choose ground that is over five hundred feet above sea level. You understand?"

We said, "Yes, we understand."

"It is high ground you need, not too open. You need trees and water, a fast-flowing river to purify the vibration.

Seek and you *will* find!

Be aware of us as you seek and we will impress you. This is *very* important. We need you both in the right area. It is essential for the completion of the solar work."

Dudley then asked about a possible job in the area. The Teacher replied with these words: "Earthly work will be found for you in the right area. Use your wits and make a way. No matter what, it will grow from that. Do not feel that a simple task is unworthy; it will lead to more interesting, worthwhile work. You have so much to give at all levels. Advance slowly and in complete trust. The army of the White Brotherhood are by your side. We use these terms because with your past history and military lives, you will understand them. You are now on active service. God bless you."

The Teacher then ended the message with words of love and gratitude to both of us.

The clarity and speed of this message was exciting. It certainly boosted our self-confidence and helped us to realise how exact the solar work was going to be. We were impressed by the direct comments and instructions regarding the landscape and height above sea level. It was all so practical and positive. Certainly a great deal was going to happen in a short time. I was particularly interested in the comment about directing us to the right area in which to find a dwelling. My experience of finding Huish

Champflower on the map and the response I had felt, combined with the Teacher's remarks about the 'old wisdom' and vibrations, urged me to ask a few more questions of my own. So, two days later, I settled down to make contact with the Group through the Teacher. The contact was immediate and went as follows:

"We greet you, Golden One.

The way is getting clearer; make plans for the move to the new dwelling.

Q: Will it happen soon?

A: Yes, it will be accelerated. Keep to the north-eastern area above Tiverton. This is the area with the Old Wisdom. The Brendon Hills. It is here that the light can enter.

Q: Why the Brendon Hills area?

A: Because it was once an area of many wise people who understood nature's ways and the healing and care of the soil. We need you in this area again, for much solar work. We say: keep close to the ways of wild nature. Plants, trees, soil and all the beasts need your help. Your help will be by the *written* word combined with intuitive action.

Q: What of Huish Champflower, on the edge of the Brendon Hills? Is it too soon to ask?

A: It is the right place for your work.

Q: Shall I try using the pendulum on the map to find the right place?

A: Yes, you will find it most helpful. We see trees, water and open moor close by. The house will be very old and rather larger than you expected. The space is needed for future work and as a sanctuary. The house will be built of stone. Do *not* hesitate at its size. Much will take place there and many will join you there from time to time. Your work is *with* the natural world. It's always best out of doors. Here you will find the Hill of Wisdom.

We go now. God bless you. We all love you. Teacher."

This message with its detailed comments was enlightening, almost disconcertingly so. It was wonderful to get confirmation of Huish Champflower, but I was indeed surprised at the size of the dwelling they described. We had been asking the West Country agents to send us particulars of small cottages! Risdon,

Tarr & Morle of Wiveliscombe had just sent us a large sheaf of details of several cottages in the area and we were working our way through them. Some were almost derelict and all were of the two-up-three-down variety. Thus, the message and the size of the property we had requested would certainly make the quest for the 'right dwelling' a stimulating one! I decided to search through the advertisements of West Country properties for sale which appeared every week in the *Daily Mail*.

A few days after the message of April 4th we laid the map out on the dining room table and I worked my pendulum over it. Sure enough, in the Huish Champflower area it swung into a strong and steady rhythmic movement. The message and the pendulum agreed. All movement seemed to be converging on Huish Champflower. On April 10th Dudley visited the estate agent in Lewes from whom we had purchased The Warren five years previously to inform Mr Hunt, the land agent, of our desire to put our house up for immediate sale. Their Mr Colvin visited us on the 14th to make arrangements to advertise the property. He took a good look around and we gave him various photographs. We also discussed the asking price.

On the 18th Mr Colvin called again to finalise arrangements and fix a price. On Saturday April 26th a couple by the name of Hammond who lived in nearby Hurstpierpoint called to view the property. We liked them very much, and on Tuesday the 29th they made an offer which we accepted. Events had certainly been accelerated, as the Group had commented to me in the April 4th message. A few days later I saw an advertisement in the *Daily Mail*. It had been inserted by Risdon, Tarr & Morle of Wiveliscombe, advertising a property known as 'Gauth House' in Huish Champflower which was due to come up for auction on June 3rd. It was described as an 'attractive freehold detached period country residence'. In the small photograph attached, it looked very old and rather large. Could this be the right one—the dwelling we were looking for? A bubbling excitement filled my mind. I went straight to Dudley and asked him to telephone the agents requesting them to post particulars to us without delay. A rather startled Mr Tarr took Dudley's call and said, "But, Mr Tod, this is a much larger property than the others we have sent you—you do realise this?" Dudley replied, "I do, but please send the details." Mr Tarr readily agreed and the auction particulars arrived promptly.

Gauth House was indeed rather large and very old—in fact it was a Ministry Listed building of architectural and historical interest—and the photograph attached to the auction brochure showed a long, low building resting peacefully in a wild garden. We absorbed all these particulars in complete silence. The house was part Tudor and part early Georgian. On the ground floor was an entrance hall with a spiral staircase and a cloakroom, a withdrawing room and a dining room, two large kitchens (from one a back staircase led upstairs), a wide slype and a large dairy. Upstairs were seven rooms and a bathroom. In the courtyard by the kitchens was a double-chambered stone well fed by a spring. A barn acted as a double garage with a stable beside it, complete with mounting block. A greenhouse was attached to the back of the barn. The whole property was protected by old stone walls and the gardens were on two levels. So much for the two-up-three-down we had thought of!

I read the particulars over and over again, and each time I found myself becoming more and more entranced by it all. Would it really be within our means? My experience with the purchasing of The Warren made me sure that if it was to be our new dwelling, then it would be. We started making plans to visit the area and look at all the properties including Gauth House. Accordingly, we decided to book into a small guest house at Cove for a week from May 16th to the 21st from whence we could visit all the properties the agents in Minehead and Wiveliscombe had sent us. It would be a good centre from which to radiate out on our quest. Suddenly, however, I remembered the message of April 2nd we had received stressing the importance of our new dwelling being on high ground at least five hundred feet above sea level. We had the map with the contours marked on it, but where exactly did Gauth House lie?

Dudley telephoned an even more startled Mr Tarr to enquire as to the position of Gauth House in Huish Champflower. Mr Tarr replied at once: "Oh, it's on the top of Tanner's Hill on the high ground. The house is exactly on the C of Huish Champflower on the Ordnance Survey map. The village and the church all lie on the crown of the hill." Dudley thanked him and said we were planning to come and visit all the properties he had sent us between May 16th and 21st. Mr Tarr's cheerful voice on the other end of the line said, "I look forward to meeting you both," then he rang off. We opened the O.S. map again to study the contours. Gauth House and Huish Champflower village lay on the seven-hundred-feet contour, rising up to one thousand feet above sea level. And the fast-flowing River Tone ran like a half-coiled snake around the base of the hill. This confirmation of the Group's comments and words of advice was like a strong hand supporting us.

On Sunday May 11th at 8:10 pm I had another short question-and-answer session with the Group through the Teacher. I felt that there was something important they wished to impart to me before we visited Huish Champflower. The session ran as follows:

"We greet you.

The Old Place is waiting for you—the house in the hidden garden. For long it has been a meeting place for much peace and light; Golden One, continue to use this peace and power to help in your solar work. You *are* needed in this area of Somerset, the Brendon Hills area. Here the light can get through easily. Do not be anxious about material things: if you will work with us, we will give you so much help on the earthly level. Do not forget that you are our link and channel. The way for Dudley will progress well.

Much work has been done to cleanse and purify the atmosphere in this 'Old House of Prayer'. The peace will enfold and uphold you as it does at The Warren. It is wide open, loving and full of the old wisdom. Exercise patience; do not try too hard or look too far ahead. Take one day at a time. Be filled with joy. We are all busy and send you love and encouragement.

God bless you now and always. Peace be with you. Teacher."

This message was very reassuring to me because I had been fearful that my own personal delight at the possibility of living at Gauth House might influence the outcome when we made our first visit on May 16th. This reassurance before the visit was indeed proof of the Group's understanding of my thoughts and fears. Again I was impressed by their choice of words to help me and encourage me to progress towards finalising the task I had undertaken with Dudley's help. In this message they had pointed out that I was a link in *their* chain, and how important it was to progress carefully, one step at a time, instead of trying to see too far ahead and thereby miss the small but important events which act as bridges to the big revelations on the journey through the Maze.

During this period of difficult decisions I received several messages of confirmation from other sensitives whom I had met through the healing work. These confirmations were like a strong arm in the dark, and I appreciated and valued them very much indeed. They helped me to maintain my detachment.

On May 16th we left home after breakfast. Kay Poulton had kindly agreed to come and stay at The Warren for the week we would be away to look after the animals and the house. We made our journey to Wiveliscombe in easy stages, reaching Mr Tarr's office in the square at 3:30 pm. He welcomed us very warmly and gave us both a long look before telling us that Mrs Redwood who lived in Wayside Cottage near Gauth House was acting as caretaker and keeper of the keys, as the property had been empty for a whole year. He had advised her of our possible arrival and she would show us around.

As we drove out of Wiveliscombe towards Huish Champflower, I started watching the landscape closely. We were indeed among the green hills of Somerset. Up we went to the top of Maundown Hill, then down again to cross the River Tone by the winding, old stone bridge known as Washbattle Bridge, with its mill and house close to the curve of the road. Then up again towards Tanner's Hill and Huish Champflower. The hills around us were all clad in large plantations of trees—beech, larch and pine—which flowed down to the lane, sheltering it with great boughs of varied green. On the other side, small green fields bordered the river, looking lush and green. The air was moist and fresh. What an enchanting landscape it was!

As we climbed the last curve up Tanner's Hill and reached its crown, the high stone walls of Gauth House lay on our right. Dudley slowed down, saw the entrance and carefully drove into the yard. We had arrived.

Mrs Redwood must have been looking out for us because she came bustling into the yard just as we were getting out of the car. Gauth House turned its back firmly onto the road. Only the back door, a recently inserted window in the big kitchen, a small window in the cloakroom downstairs and one bathroom window upstairs broke the long blank line of the house on its roadside face. The real front of the house was reached through an iron-studded oak door set in the wall which linked the house with the barn and the stables. A step with a mounting block beside it led up to the door, which had a portico above it. There was a bronze bell pull shaped like a hand and the knocker was an iron one depicting an imp with his tongue out. We stood in the yard looking around us. No garden was visible due to the walls. The yard was surrounded on two sides by an evergreen hedge over which we had a distant view of the surrounding hills and farmland.

As the wall door was locked from the inside, Mrs Redwood took us to the back door which had a deep porch with a slate floor. The big oak door was iron-studded and had a letterbox and knocker, both huge and made of cast iron. Mrs Redwood inserted the key and with a flourish opened the door. We found ourselves in a wide passage which she called the slype. Another large oak door with a small peep window was at the other end of this passage and gave access to the gardens and the well yard. We stood staring in wide-eyed surprise as she then opened another door off the passage which led into a large, low-ceilinged kitchen, complete with bread oven, a copper boiler, a vast open fireplace, a stone sink and a window looking out onto the well yard and the steps leading to the top garden. Next she opened another door on the opposite side of the passage revealing a high-roofed dairy with a skylight and a large iron-barred window high up at the far end. Around the walls were arranged slate-covered shelving made of stone which had been used to rest cream pans on—those wide, shallow vessels filled with milk which were skimmed when the cream had risen to the surface. From another smaller shelf high up on the wall had hung the skimming utensils, and down below buckets could be lodged beneath the stone shelving. In the centre of one wall which was at least 21 inches thick was a deep cupboard with gauze-covered doors and slate shelves. Mrs Redwood called it the 'delivery cupboard'—where cream and freshly-made butter was placed (it could also be used as a larder). The dairy floor was stone and even on a very hot day this room was always cool and airy.

Emerging from the dairy, we went down a narrow passage to

a door which led into an even larger kitchen with a modern sink unit, electric power points for a cooker and large storage cupboards. It also had an enormous fireplace where an Aga water heater stood. On one side of this fireplace was the back staircase leading to the upstairs rooms, whilst on the other was a walk-in airing cupboard. From this huge kitchen a door led into the dining room and then into the hall where the main staircase lay. The downstairs cloakroom was reached by a passage from the hall, and beyond it was the drawing room, a perfectly proportioned early Georgian room with two long windows with shutters and a superb carved wood fireplace and over-mantel of great size. The original Georgian front door opened from this hall, leading out to a long terrace running the whole length of the house. It was fairly obvious that this end-section of the house had been added to the original Tudor dwelling in the 18th century and, because the rooms were higher and the roof likewise, the long line of the roof was broken, combining an early Tudor aspect at the kitchen end and an early Georgian one at the other.

We opened the front door and stepped out onto the terrace, and as we turned to take a look at the house from the garden, it was quite amazing—11 beautiful windows smiled back at us as though saying: "Here it is, the house in the hidden garden which you were told about."

At the far end of the terrace was the wall with the door leading back into the yard where our car stood waiting. A further door led directly into the barn and the stables and the seclusion was complete. The whole property was enfolded and protected from the outside world. We went indoors again and climbed the main staircase to inspect the seven upstairs rooms, four of which were large double bedrooms and two smaller, with only the little window of the bathroom looking out onto the road. We amused ourselves running up one staircase and down the other. Next we went out again to explore the garden, all of which was wild and very mysterious. Roses cascaded over shrubs and trees, and laurels grew in strange shapes making delightful little arbours. My thoughts started racing away with excitement. This was all too perfect. And yet the Group's message was still unfolding before my eyes. I began to feel overawed by their love and their appreciation of what I was trying so hard to do with their help. I could sense the nature spirits around us; mentally I welcomed them and promised that if we lived here they would be free to continue their work with the trees and plants. I invoked their help. I knew that I couldn't manage without them.

As we approached the well yard outside the old kitchens, I felt the familiar tingling sensation of heightened awareness. Here was a beautiful stone-built spring well with two chambers side by side. One was for the spring to run into, the other, with two steps down into it, was the dip well from which buckets of water could be drawn for domestic work and washing. What a busy place it must have been when it was the only source of sweet water for the whole household. It had been most carefully constructed by a stonemason who understood his craft and had a natural eye for beauty and a true awareness of the infinite value of pure water. Each chamber had a barrel-shaped roof of perfectly placed stones. The spring was directed into the first chamber by a narrow chute just the right height for a water vessel to be placed beneath it. The continually running water flowed across the stone floor and through a channel into the second chamber, the dip well. Small ferns and tiny water-loving plants grew among the stones, reflecting their delicate green shades inside as well as outside the chambers. Above the well a cluster of laurels, brambles and creepers draped their branches and tendrils towards the water. The continuous sound of gently moving water and the beauty of the well's construction created an atmosphere of light, tranquillity and infinite joy. Here, closely connected with the house, were the elements of earth, air and water.

We walked back along the terrace to the front door and stood looking at the long view across the meadows towards Maundown Hill with the River Tone flowing far below us. As we looked, we saw fine white vapour rising from the water. The plantations on the lower slopes of the hill made a perfect backcloth for such a magical sight. I found it difficult to leave this tranquil old place, but we still had 16 miles to travel in order to reach Cove. We thanked Mrs Redwood for her kindness and slowly drove away in the soft evening light, arriving at our guest house in time for supper.

It had been a very long day. Doubts began to rise up almost at once. Could we really afford to purchase Gauth House? Our finances were very limited. It was much larger than even I had expected and Dudley's practical eyes had noted a number of repairs which would have to be undertaken. An auction seemed so much more final than a private sale. Fatigue tempted me to be over-anxious and negative. But I *had* seen the Old Place which the Group said was waiting for us, of this I was quite certain. They had promised us help on an earthly level if we trusted them. My trust and faith in their wisdom had to remain strong if the task was to be completed.

The next few days were hectic, with more visits to likely properties and attending two auctions to get the feel and also to note the kind of prices auctioned houses were fetching. On the Sunday we had a very pleasant day in the company of several Rosicrucians, one of whom, who owned a big furniture store in Tiverton, offered to move us when we had found a suitable house in the area. This was a great kindness which we much appreciated and did eventually take up.

The day before we left Cove to return home we visited Gauth House once again. Mrs Redwood gave us the key and we entered alone. The peace in the Old Place was like balm after all the other awful properties we had visited. Slowly we wandered about the house, looking at everything, feeling and touching. I became aware of each room as I entered it—its shape and size and the position of the windows and cupboards. I also carefully inspected and recorded the door knobs, the colour of the wallpaper, the fireplaces—everything. In one of the upstairs rooms I held my pendulum absolutely still and waited. After a few seconds it started to swing in a steady and ever-widening circle until I had difficulty in holding on to the string. I made a clear contact with the Group who responded immediately. I said, "If this is the right place for the solar work, we will endeavour to purchase it in spite of its size and state of dilapidation. Please help us. We both trust you and want to cooperate with you." The pendulum swung round even faster. The energy building up was powerful and very positive. Gradually the pendulum started to slow down and when it was still I caught it with my left hand and put it back in my pocket. The contact had been made.

Back at The Warren I still felt the tingling excitement of our visits to Gauth House. The Group's messages of April 4th and May 11th had been so completely accurate, directing our steps with such care and concern for the well-being of all. I was deeply grateful to them, but my sadness at leaving The Warren and all our local friends was very strong. It distressed me very much to leave so many loving souls who had helped us and given their friendship with such generosity. I also grieved at having to leave the house where so much had happened in the past five years. And Dudley still had no job to go to! It certainly was a trial of faith and hope. But the Group were well aware of my feelings because on Friday May 23rd, two days after our return from Somerset, I had the following session with them:

"We greet you.

We say to you, Golden One, you have followed our promptings—the Old Place on the hill is indeed your new dwelling. The well contains the living water; it comes from the pure source —use it.

We say you will be well guarded during this final period and the purchase of the house. We need you both in this area. The way for Dudley will be on the lines he knows well—figures.

Do not grieve; all partings are difficult. You will be surrounded by the Light in the new dwelling. Work with Pan and his kingdoms. Look ahead to this new slice of your life.

This task which you will complete with Dudley's help is also part of a much larger project of communication and cooperation with the natural world, now being undertaken in various parts of the British Isles. All are linked with you. You are *all* part of the whole. But each link is necessary for the project to function with maximum energy, harmony and goodwill.

Now you know, do not overtax your physical strength. We are busy in the area and send you much love."

I thanked them, most sincerely, for all the help they had given me, but we were still very concerned about the purchase price, the reserve figure the owner of Gauth House would put on it for the auction. The Teacher replied to my query in these words:

"That will be attended to. The friends are close, they will impress. We say, have a joyful heart, Golden One, the quest is almost finished. You are on the Path of Light. Follow it step by step. We need your pen. Peace be with you. Teacher."

This was a profound message. I read it through many times in a quiet, meditative way. I needed to feel my way carefully right through it. Being part of a larger project was very stimulating as well as revealing. Indeed, it made me acutely aware of how we are all part of the whole cosmos and how important is each link in the chain of cosmic consciousness. This realisation of the wonder and power of the natural world (and all its kingdoms) was almost overwhelming. I felt intense gratitude and joy at being allowed to partake in such an important project. To re-create the true awareness between human beings and the kingdoms of the natural world was so dear to my heart, I was willing to pay any price to help achieve it.

I was conscious of a link with Eileen and Peter Caddy and Dorothy Maclean in the Findhorn Garden and of an ancient and abiding connection with Robert Ogilvie Crombie, through his contacts with Pan and Pan's subjects. I also felt strong links with Glastonbury and Chalice Well, and with the islands of Iona, Orkney and the Outer Hebrides. Areas of the South Downs were also close to me, as were parts of Hampshire and, of course, Somerset.

From a friend I received the name and address of an organisation known as the Soil Association, which had its head office in Suffolk. The aims of the association were to promote organic farming and gardening, and to reveal the ultimate harm which would result from the use of modern chemical fertilisers and poison sprays. They urged people everywhere to show a respect for the living soil and the environment, to appreciate its intrinsic value, and to work with nature to create a real balance between humanity's needs and the care and well-being of the soil. In other words, they were advocating the very important merits of good husbandry which had been the norm before modern science dangled its promises of a vastly increased yield by the use of intensive chemical fertilisers—a temptation which dazzled the human eye and urged human greed towards larger and larger crops.

I felt totally in harmony with the Soil Association's aims. We wrote to them to ask whether there might be Soil Association groups in other parts of the British Isles. Back came the reply —yes, indeed, there were several groups, and they kindly listed them for us. To our delight we saw that West Somerset had a

Soil Association group and that their meetings were held at the Constitutional Rooms in Wiveliscombe! These contacts and communications were wonderfully reassuring. I had the feeling that we were being urged onwards at an ever-increasing rate.

On Monday June 2nd Dudley drove by himself to Wiveliscombe to attend the Gauth House auction due to take place the following afternoon, June 3rd. He had previously booked in for bed and breakfast at a small guest house close to the main square, so as to be near to both the estate agent and the Constitutional Rooms, where the auction would be held at 3 pm.

In the evening he telephoned me to relate the day's adventures and activities. On arrival at Wiveliscombe he had contacted a local builder and together they had visited Gauth House to estimate the cost of the essential repairs required. After a careful inspection, and much figuring out with pencil and paper, the builder gave Dudley an estimated figure of £500. Dudley felt that the builder was a man of integrity and would not try to push up the price if he eventually did the work, so a provisional agreement was made, subject of course to our being able to purchase. We knew we had to be very careful as our total finances were limited to £5,000. Now that he had this estimate, Dudley knew his limit on any bid would be £4,500. He questioned the builder, who felt the house might go for around £3,000. He also gathered some more information from the local post office and other centres of interested gossip and found a consensus of opinion which thought the house *might* fetch anything between £3,000 and £4,000. Most of them had known the property for years and all felt it would need a lot doing to it. Eagerly they vied with one another in making helpful suggestions, but they all ended up by saying, "You never can tell at an auction—some people go quite mad!"

Dudley's voice rang with laughter as he recounted this over the telephone to me, and he had obviously enjoyed his day out in West Somerset. He sounded confident and cheerful. I too felt confident and very hopeful. The Group's messages had all been so positive. Finally we arranged that Dudley would telephone me as soon as he could after the auction to let me know the result. We were both excited by the day's events. We sent loving messages to one another, and he rang off.

Afterwards, I sat in the garden, with the dog and the cats

pottering about contentedly and rolling in the soft grass; occasionally they made adventurous little darts into the big, sweetly scented box hedges that were their private jungle. It was a beautiful evening, clear and still; sounds from the woods and fields blended with my thoughts, and presently the spirit of the place gently enfolded me, helping me to come to terms with the duality of sorrow at leaving The Warren and joy at the prospect of journey's end.

Until now, my married life had been a series of moves; we had seldom stayed anywhere longer than a few years. In Somerset would we, at last, have reached the end of the journey and found the place where the task was to be completed? Oh, how I longed to complete this task. The Group in all their messages seemed so sure. I lay still on the grass with closed eyes. My intuition, fully extended in this powerful place, echoed a loud 'yes'.

As the light slowly faded in the garden, a blackbird sang his evening song, then busily occupied himself with settling down for the night. Bats flew out from under the cottage tiles. An owl called, far into the wood, and faint sounds from the valley below drifted upwards. The dog was sound asleep and the cats curled up into tight little balls, also deep in sleep. Contentment filled my being. I felt completely at one with the natural world. I too was falling asleep on the soft, dew-wet grass.

***

Tuesday June 3rd—the day of the Gauth House auction:
I spent the morning in the woods and on the downland. I moved around quietly admiring the beauty of the wild flowers and the trees. As I wandered, an adder, curled up on a grass mound, watched as I passed. Undisturbed by me, it did not rear up or glide away, but continued to enjoy its warm sunbath in peace. I have always found that moving slowly through the landscape, just looking and listening, and sometimes halting for minutes on end, is very revealing. Shy woodland creatures often show themselves, busy around their natural life, seemingly quite unaware of my presence. This acceptance is very precious to me. As I slowly emerged onto the downland, the clear bright light reflecting off the chalky soil dazzled my eyes. This intense brilliance reminded me that someone had once said the light on

the South Downs is similar to the light in Greece. On this particular morning I felt a strong link with the Greek landscape—ancient memories were stirring in my unconscious, and I reflected again on the messages Dorothy Robins had brought me, and on the part The Warren was playing to help me on my journey. As I gazed at the surrounding woods and downland, I said a profound thank you to all Pan's subjects in the elemental kingdom and especially to the pure spirit of nature, Pan himself. By early afternoon, I had returned to The Warren to be close to the telephone. Just before 3 pm—the time of the auction—I sat down to wait.

At 3:45 pm the telephone rang. Dudley's voice was full of distress as he told me that Gauth House had been sold for £5,000 to a local farmer named Vance, acting for his mother who lived in Ireland. The farmer had bid up to the reserve figure and we had lost. He then went on to tell me that in the morning he had called at Mr Tarr's office to ask a few more questions. Mr Tarr was out but expected back shortly, so Dudley decided to wait. Presently the telephone rang and the young clerk who answered listened for a few seconds and then said, "Yes, Mrs Gurney. I understand. The reserve figure is £5,000. I will tell Mr Tarr as soon as he returns. Thank you and goodbye."

Dudley knew at once that Mrs Gurney was the owner of Gauth House, and now, by being in the office at that particular time, he knew the reserve price *before* the auction took place. His only hope, therefore, had been that no one would bid up to the reserve price, and after the auction he could offer £4,500 and it might be accepted. But it was obviously not to be. Dudley's voice sounded very weary and forlorn. Meanwhile, I was trying hard to keep calm. All I could manage to say was, "Thank you, darling, for phoning. Come back as soon as you can tomorrow. I will go and get in touch with the Group. There *must* be a reason for this. Thank you so much for all you have done to help."

Automatically I went upstairs to my table and sat down. For a long time I could do nothing but sit still. Gradually I began to feel calmer. I said my prayers of protection and invocation and waited, pen in hand. Very slowly the following words came through:

"We greet you.

The Old Place *is* waiting for you. Have faith."

Nothing more came. I looked at the words in utter disbelief. I read them again, and waited, but there was nothing else. I became perplexed and bewildered and then my very human anger rose up. How could the Old Place be waiting for us? It had just been sold at an auction to someone else. What had gone wrong? Had we not worked with the Group as requested? Had we not carefully followed their instructions? My anger flew all over the place, in all directions. Suddenly, I burst into floods of tears. They broke the tension and after a while I felt calm again, ashamed of my violent outburst. After a period of quiet the Teacher very slowly conveyed the following words:

"Indeed, the Old Place is waiting for you. Golden One, continue to visit the area. Seek and you will find. We all love you and need your pen. God bless you. Teacher."

The gentle love that came with these simple and extremely wise words filled my heart with renewed joy. I felt supported and comforted, my human emotions understood and my stupid outburst forgiven. We were *needed* in this area—of course we would go on looking for a dwelling among the Brendon Hills.

And so we did. We made four more visits to view properties in the area. On the fourth visit Mr Tarr gave us particulars of a cottage called 'Priestlands' near Huish Champflower. It was on high ground known as Bittiscombe Hill. He gave us the key, asking that we would return it after we had looked around. The date was July 15th and we had to move out of The Warren by August 20th, when the Hammonds would move in. Time was getting short!

Priestlands turned out to be a delightful cottage with only two main drawbacks—it was surrounded by a pig farm and Dudley could stand upright in only one room. We would just have to go on seeking.

On our return to Wiveliscombe I remained in the car, which we had parked in the public car park, and Dudley took the key back to Mr Tarr's office. As I sat there I began to feel excited—I felt sure something was going to happen, and the longer Dudley was away, the more excited I became. Then I saw him striding across the car park, waving his arms, his eyes sparkling with suppressed excitement. Something *had* happened. I threw the car door open and he jumped in, crying, "We've got it! We've got it after all! Gauth House is ours!"

It transpired that just as Dudley was handing back the key, the telephone rang. It was Farmer Vance to say his mother was unable to get her money out from Ireland after all, and would Mr Tarr please put Gauth House back on the market at once. Mr Tarr turned to Dudley and said, "Would you like to make an offer, Mr Tod?"

Dudley offered our £4,500 which Farmer Vance immediately accepted. He was more than willing to drop £500 for such a quick sale. Dudley then said we would need to move into Gauth House on August 20th even if the contract had not been finalised by then. Farmer Vance again agreed. He had, after all, already paid the £500 deposit after the auction and Dudley's £4,500 offer would free him of any further payments to Mrs Gurney. He was obviously delighted to have made such a quick sale and thus saved his mother from financial embarrassment.

So the Old House *had* been waiting for us all the time, just as the Group's messages had promised. I expressed a loud and heartfelt 'thank you' to one and all as we sat in the car in Wiveliscombe's main car park. This experience was a marvellous confirmation and proof of the trust and cooperation which had been built up between the Group and ourselves. We felt confident about our future work in West Somerset. My own joy was limitless. The golden cord was unbroken—we were all united in love and cosmic energy.

During our final period at The Warren we received several messages from the Group through the Teacher, urging us to get ourselves well established in Gauth House and Dudley in a steady job *before* starting on the solar work. We noted this advice with great care, realising the importance of 'correct timing'.

Another lovely and quite unexpected happening occurred before we left The Warren. The Badmin family gave us a wonderful farewell party at their home in Bignor, near Pulborough. All the Rosicrucian members had gathered together to wish us well in our new dwelling—the Old House of Prayer—in West Somerset.

It was a perfect summer's day as we sat together enjoying the beauty of the garden with its dramatic backcloth of Bury Hill shimmering in the distance. The warmth of the sun and the loving friendship which surrounded us made it a day to be long remembered and talked about. Other friends came to The Warren to wish us happiness and success.They brought us gifts we really did not deserve, and showered us with their love which we received with joy tinged, naturally, with sadness at the parting, but happily lightened by the prospect of their coming to visit us in West Somerset at some later time.

Chapter 4
Somerset and the Appointed Place

The move to Gauth House was accomplished in good weather and with the minimum of fuss.

It took us several weeks to get used to the change of altitude—we were now living about 400 feet nearer to the sun than we had been at The Warren. The landscape was quite different and so was the size of the house. We were also far less isolated than we had been: now I could easily walk to the shop and the post office, the church and the public house. It took a lot of getting used to.

On the third evening after arrival, I wandered through the wild gardens hoping to meet the nature spirits and to reassure them that they would be free of disturbances by us. They gave me a beautiful welcome, surrounding me with colour and light and happy, peaceful intentions. I knew then that all would be well for all of us. We were amongst powerful and loving friends who belonged to the elemental kingdom. I recognised them and they, I believe, recognised me. Harmony was established.

The Wiveliscombe builder fulfilled his promises and completed the essential repairs in a masterly way. We were indeed fortunate to have his careful crafstmanship. He and his workers seemed to love the Old House and understood its needs. When he had completed his work, we got very busy fixing carpets and curtains, arranging the furniture and various fittings, hanging pictures and mirrors and probing the depths of the large cupboards looking for mice and spiders. At first it seemed strange to have so many large rooms but they soon became filled up with books and treasures of all kinds which we had brought from The Warren. When everything was finally arranged, our good friends from Sussex duly came a-visiting. We took great pleasure in showing them the house, the Brendon Hills and all the beautiful places in the area. Their delighted responses were most encouraging and it really was lovely to have the rooms in which to accommodate them all.

During the 19 years we have lived in this Old House of Prayer so many different people have come to stay, some for a rest, some for sanctuary, and some to help with the solar work—just as the early messages from the Group said they would. It has been our joy and our delight to welcome and care for them as well as sharing the Old Place with them.

As soon as he could, Dudley started attending the Rosicrucian meetings at Cove. He told me that the membership was wide and varied and, like the Brighton members, they were a group of very interesting personalities from differing social backgrounds. Each had an especial gift or vocation which they used with integrity and great perception. Their personal kindness towards us was full of grace and we deeply appreciated all the help they gave us. On one occasion they invited me to join Dudley at one of their banquets held in a hotel near Exeter. It was a fascinating experience and very exciting because it was there that I met Joan Tanner, their group master for that year, and immediately recognised her. Joan's stature, although short and very slender, was full of a powerful inner strength. Her whole being was swift, direct, determined, all superbly balanced and controlled in a gentle, loving way. I recognised the Grecian link: Joan was the third member of the triangle needed to complete the solar work. When the time was right to start the work, I knew that she would join us. Before this work started, however, Joan came to Gauth House and had a question-and-answer session. I also did several by post for her and the Group confirmed that she was indeed the third member of the triangle. Joan's hobby is archaeology—digging up the past—and she is very good at it.

Another recognition from the Greek incarnation came when I met Dr Frederick Drummond Robb, a healer with stupendous gifts which he used freely to help all manner of people. He had a small clinic in Dulverton when we first met him; later he moved to Minehead. In 1973 he saved the sight of my right eye. He also cleared and dispersed the post-clinical rheumatic fever symptoms which had tormented me on and off since I contracted this illness when I was 15. I was profoundly grateful to him for these miracles which he performed with such skill. When I thanked him, he smiled, looked straight at me and said, "Well, you did save my life in ancient Greece; now I help you in return!" He said it so directly and so simply, I knew it must be true. We embraced each other in mutual recognition. These eternal links, when recognised, enrich our human lives a hundredfold. They glorify creation by revealing the truly spiritual meaning of love in action.

Not long after our arrival at Gauth House, we joined the West Somerset Soil Association and attended their meetings in the Constitutional Rooms at Wiveliscombe, where we made many new and valuable friendships among the members. They were mostly small working farmers with a tremendous enthusiasm for and love of their age-old craft. They were alarmed at the way modern chemical farming was disturbing the natural patterns of nature. The talks and discussions, as well as the farm walks which the Committee arranged for the members' interest, were very good indeed and stimulated a great deal of debate during and after the meetings. Some of course were better than others, but after each meeting I found that I had learned something new or seen something in a new light.

The organic attitude towards the animal, vegetable and mineral kingdoms is the only safe one. Conservation and respect for the natural world will, we hope, gradually become more widely recognised and accepted. It is a balance between need and greed, not an easy proposition in our ever-increasingly 'high-tech' world where speed, size, quantity and high profits rule.

The following year Dudley was asked by the West Somerset Soil Association Committee if he would take on the secretaryship—and he did. Soon I was drawn in to make cakes for the meetings and help with the catering. We also started a monthly 'bring and buy' market in the big kitchen of Gauth House. It was great fun and a wonderful way to get to know our neighbours and the local farming fraternity.

In November 1969 (three months after our arrival) Dudley was offered a job in the accounts department of a large factory in Wellington, some nine miles away. (A job with figures, just as the Group message had said!) Dudley stayed a year with the factory accounts department and then was offered a job with a firm of chartered accountants, first in Bridgewater and then in

Taunton, where he remained working contentedly until his retirement in 1980.

***

As I look back over the years spent journeying through the Maze, I realise with awe and wonder just how much cooperation, love and understanding the Group have offered me through their messages (whose consistency is truly amazing). How accurate they were about Gauth House and that Dudley's 'bread and butter' job in Somerset would be with figures. How wise and correct was their advice to get ourselves really well established in the Old House and Dudley in a steady job *before* starting on the solar ray work. Then again the Group's faith in me and my pen, in spite of my human weaknesses and doubts, has been unwavering and firm as a rock. Their love and trust have created a clear channel of infinite power for good. United we are and always will be. The pure light of cosmic consciousness transcends all, unites all. Humankind and the four kingdoms (animal, vegetable, mineral and elemental) who *share* the Planet Earth are all part of the whole.

Cosmic laws are indeed God's laws. Once again I am reminded of the full impact of those words spoken so long ago by my maternal grandmother—*"Cherie, l'on adore que Dieu"* —and the stunning awareness of reality which they revealed to me, that all religions are human-made, but the universe is God-given.

In one of his messages to me, Roc expressed the following words:

"This task which you undertook—and promised to complete—is always difficult to define because by most human beings it is unseen. If you had made an article, written a poem, started a community or painted a picture, it could be seen by all and commented upon. Opinions could be expressed and shared regarding it. Cosmic forces, unnoticed and invisible to the naked eye, are much more subtle and difficult to accept. But they *are*. They can vitally affect an area, a plant, a person, an animal and a whole landscape. Those like you who work with the cosmic forces and the elemental kingdom are always looked at with a certain amount of doubt. As Kurmos said, 'If they could *see* us, they would love us.' Indeed, many do and many more will as time goes by. Cooperation with the elemental kingdom cannot be ignored. Pan *is*.

Please remember these comments. They will give you encouragement. Each of the kingdoms needs their 'wise ones' to help them balance the forces of *homo sapiens*. You are indeed one of us. God bless you."

These comments of Roc's did indeed give me encouragement and strength. They made sense of so much that had happened over the years. They also revived old memories which led me to recall this poem written by my beloved friend and mentor, Gerald Bullett, entitled 'Then and Now'.

In my green leaf I lacked tongue to tell
Delight or dread Time, the living moment,
Ever-expanding bubble sunned and mooned
Containing earth and heaven, was then home,
Lit by flower's glory and star's bloom.

Now, exiled from those immortal days,
The bubble time adrift in darkening air and
Soon to be pricked, I trace their joys and fears,
And marvel to see my boughs, iron bare,
Scatter the grass with dry leaves of praise.

The first time I read his poem, Gerald told me, "I wrote it after observing an old tree just above Turkey Island (the name of a place close to his home in East Harting, Sussex). This old tree seemed to express so well the journey through life. The youthful sapling dancing in the wind, drinking the rain, its roots slowly spreading ever outwards, expanding its growth. Then the mature tree, protecting and nurturing the life around it. Then the gradual aging and the loss of vitality and strength. Finally, the marvel of continued usefulness through decay and death, with nothing wasted.

"Praise is praise of the Earth, the planet, with its wondrous ability to re-create itself in spite of the human love for destruction and change, which is invariably made in the name of glorious progress!"

This fascinating poem and Gerald's comments, so penetratingly expressed, bring to an end these brief glimpses of my long journey through the Maze because, in a quite magical way, they reflect so many of my own feelings as I travelled along.

***

In the spring of 1971 our work with the solar rays—the quarterly Light ceremonies—began.

In the winter of 1982 the work was finally and successfully completed. It was then I saw quite clearly that our task had been to cooperate in harmony with the natural forces concerned with the fusion of solar energy with earth energy—a blend of natural science and spirituality which enables a balanced and beneficial growth to be maintained in nature. It links all the four kingdoms and brings harmony and understanding to all life in the area. Our work also specifically linked Elworthy Henge and its sun temple with the Glastonbury Tor.

PART TWO
THE ARC OF LIGHT

THE TASK

You have a duty to perform . . .
Do anything else, do any number of things,
occupy your time fully, and yet,
if you do not do this task,
all your time will have been wasted.

Jalaludin Rumi (1207-1273)

NOW

In this inscrutable moment
Stand we face to face
With That for which no words are
Yet must be spoken,
That which, unformed, half-seen,
Must be conveyed.

Steeped in illusion of mortality
How shall we demonstrate
That we are Life at the core—
Instantly—now?
And thro' intensified experience raise
Sloth of unawareness
Into high-charged environment?

Shall we not call, using
No cumbrous instruments
But frequencies Known only to the Wise
Thro' immemorial Time—
That they may speak—and we,
At last, may hear?

(Written by the Scottish poet Margaret Forbes, who died in 1968)

Chapter 5
Messages of Instruction

As the messages convey, the patterning of our work with the solar rays built up slowly and steadily over the years. This allowed people who were interested to follow without being led. Spiritual patterning enabled each one to make their own contribution, which is far more valuable than blind obedience. It may be slow, but its final results are pure and without guile.

As the messages predicted, many people came to share the quarterly Light ceremonies with us. Each came of their own free will and came again, or left, according to their own life patterns.

These quarterly Light ceremonies were indeed joyful and full of aspirations. We took great care before the ceremony and on our way to the site to be in harmony and balance with all life.

The ritual was performed with intense concentration, cooperation and dedication. The energy thus created was very great. After each ceremony we all enjoyed a simple communal meal in the large kitchen in Gauth House. Each member brought a contribution and it was wonderful to see the big, bare table quickly become covered with gifts of delicious flans, crusty brown bread, butter and a variety of cheese, fruits and wines. Salads in big bowls and bunches of flowers in high vases made a perfect decoration. In winter, I made a large saucepan full of soup to go with the bread and cheese. These magical meals were always accompanied by much laughter, story telling and fascinating conversation.

We always ended the afternoon by sitting around the fire in the drawing room, drinking cups of fragrant tea and talking. Many friendships were forged and new interests discussed, and many exciting and unexpected links were discovered as we chatted happily together. I was always very conscious of the unseen Group's gentle presence—they seemed to blend with us in a subtle and lovely way. It was with their cooperation, their energy and their love and patience that we finally and successfully completed the task. During the 12 years it took us to do the work, our much beloved Joan Tanner missed only two ceremonies and Dudley one (when Joan Tanner read the Great Invocation). I managed to be present at all the ceremonies.

No ceremony ever had to be cancelled because of bad weather. All the 49 visits which we made over the 12 years were successfully accomplished—a truly amazing confirmation of the exactness of the Group's message given to us on Friday 19th March 1971, part of which read as follows: "Do not be concerned about the earthly weather—that will be taken care of."

In December 1970 we received the following message from the Group, through the Teacher:

"We greet you.

As we have told you before, the solar ray work you will be undertaking is part of a large project that will come about gradually. It will not be an explosion of excitement! It will be slow, steady work with much thought and effort needed to get the angles right. It is the angle at which the ray enters the Earth's atmosphere which is of vital importance.

You have the old knowledge from your temple work—remember the exact placing of the shaft of light in the centre of the triangle? The work you will presently be doing is on similar lines. It will be the bringing of the divine power down into the Earth's atmosphere at exactly placed Light points.

This preparatory work is needed to enable the rays to enter the Earth's atmosphere at exactly the right angle and, after they have fused with the Earth's energy, to radiate outwards. These Light points on the high ground will act as springboards which the rays can rebound off and spread outwards to a great distance doing the work they are intended to do.

Golden One, the teachings you have been receiving are a 'remembering' of the work you started to do before (in the late Bronze Age) and now you will complete it. It is a cooperation with us to make the ground ready for the rays to fall into. We work here in eternity—you work on the Planet Earth where you are presently incarnated. You can, as you know, raise the vibrations of an area, and when this is completed the healing rays can come through strongly to do the work for which they are intended. As you know, vibrations have varying powers, so it is according to the balanced preparation the ground receives that the benefit can be judged. Your work will be to prepare the ground at several Light points (high ground) by using the ritual which we will tell you about when the time is right to start the solar ray work. Many will join you as the work progresses.

God's love surrounds you both.

Teacher."

In January 1971 it was made clear to me by the Group that the time was approaching when we would start on the solar ray work because:

1. We were now firmly established in the Old House.
2. Dudley had a steady job.
3. My links with the Group, through the Teacher, had been well tested and proven.
4. My cosmic consciousness was now sufficiently developed to allow the solar ray work to begin.

We prepared ourselves by concentrating on the true meaning of the work, and the part we must play in preparing the ground at various Light points, the locations of which the Group would give us at the appropriate time. We realised this work would need careful study of the area of the Brendon Hills, so we purchased a 2.5-inch Ordnance Survey map—Sheet ST 03. As I studied this detailed map, seeking the high ground and observing the contours, I was conscious of a large number of tumuli and barrows—this had obviously been a very important area in the Bronze Age. Looking more closely, I noted that Elworthy Barrows were on the highest ground. These barrows held my attention: with pen and ruler I started to join these Light points together with straight lines, and quickly found that they formed triangles. Barrows and tumuli had clearly been placed with great care and mathematical precision as Light points, connected by what are now called ley lines. The Brendon Hills were indeed a powerful area!

We were told that the solar ray ceremonies we would perform should take place four times a year—in spring, summer, autumn and winter—and that the following ritual must be observed on each occasion:

"Approach the selected Light points with clear, uncluttered and harmonious minds.

On arrival at the exact spot, members are to stand facing the magnetic North (if three or more, to stand in the shape of a triangle, the apex of the triangle pointing towards the magnetic North).

At mid-day (noon) on the appointed day, Dudley is to read the Great Invocation in a loud, clear voice.

Golden One, standing at the apex of the triangle, facing the magnetic North, is to perform the blessing actions as the Great Invocation is read.

The blessing actions are to be performed as follows:

Hands clasped across the chest, then arms slowly raised, with the palms of the hands resting together in a vertical position, until the arms are stretched directly upwards above the head; then arms spread out, the palms to form a chalice, held thus for a few seconds; then stretching the arms out horizontally on each side of the body, with the right-hand palm facing upwards and the left-hand palm facing downwards, to form an unbroken flow of energy from the atmosphere into the earth. At the end of the recital of the Great Invocation, the arms to be returned with hands clasped across the chest.

The reading of the Great Invocation and the blessing actions —this unity of thought, actions and words—will mark the spot where the solar rays can enter.

The Great Invocation: when reading the words 'May Christ return to Earth', it is the Christ consciousness in all life which is being invoked to assist in the cleansing and healing of the maltreated environment, by balancing the vibrations. During this ritual the concentrated thought of all the members is essential. The unity of one-pointed thought, held in harmony for a short period of time, builds up a very powerful energy. This built-up energy marks the ground and acts as a magnet to draw down the solar rays."

The Great Invocation

From the point of Light within the mind of God
Let light stream forth into the minds of men.
Let Light descend on Earth.

From the point of Love within the Heart of God
Let love stream forth into the hearts of men.
May Christ return to Earth.

From the centre where the Will of God is known
Let purpose guide the little wills of men—
The purpose which the Masters know and serve.

From the centre which we call the race of men
Let the Plan of Love and Light work out.
And may it seal the door where evil dwells.

Let Light and Love and Power restore the Plan on Earth.

Chapter 6
Reports on Ceremonies and Their Venues 1971-1973

We were filled with awe and wonder at the extent of the faith and trust placed in us by the Group. We renewed our promise to cooperate to the best of our ability.

In February 1971 we experienced a tremendous feeling of anticipation and excitement. Something was going to happen and soon.

At 8:15 pm on Friday 19th March 1971, the message we had been waiting for came through:

"We greet you.

Welcome Dudley and Golden One. Here we begin on the solar ray work. You have the map ready. Shall we start or have you a question first?"

Dudley said, "We do not have a question but I would like to express my gratitude to the Group for all their help regarding my new job."

The teacher replied:

"Well said; thank you. We are so pleased with the way in which you have accepted your new work with figures, as we told you. Now to the map! We would request you and our Golden One to proceed as follows:

Look at your map of the Brendon Hills area—there we would like you to start on the work of cleansing the soil and preparing the way for the solar rays to come through. Go first to one of the highest spots in the area which you will find is marked as Tripp Barrows. From this point, find the exact centre of the contour (you will note that the barrow is not in the centre of the contour). At this exact point, we would request you both to stand facing the magnetic North and at 12 noon on the date of the Vernal Equinox (March 21st) Dudley reads the Great Invocation and our Golden One undertakes the blessing actions.

This simple ritual, which we have already told you about, will enable the ray to come through clearly at midnight and radiate out to the surrounding ground, preparing it for the sowing of the seeds which takes place during the Vernal Equinox period.

Seven days later please proceed to Elworthy Barrows. Once again find the exact centre of its contour and at this point, on the stroke of noon, Dudley reads the Great Invocation and Golden One undertakes the blessing actions. Always remember to face the magnetic North—this makes a complete circle for us and we can work with you through this circle.

We need you to make these two visits during this Vernal Equinox period to mark clearly these two important Light points at the start of our combined solar ray work. In future you will visit just the one Light point which we will tell you of at each of the four seasons of the Vernal Equinox, Summer Solstice, Autumn Equinox and the Winter Solstice.

At each Light point, as we give it to you, find the exact centre of the contour on the map and work from that position, always facing the magnetic North.

This work you are undertaking is needed and needs to be exact. It is cosmic work. We undertake it with you in unity and with love. We will be close as you work. Do not be concerned about the earthly weather—that will be taken care of. The joy with which we give you these instructions is indeed great. Together you are starting this work; presently many others will join you and the strength will grow accordingly. Have you any questions to ask?"

We said, "No".

"You understand the instructions fully?"

We said, "Yes, thank you. It is very clear, and we have this recorded message to guide us."

The Teacher ended the message as follows:

"God bless your work. You will be surrounded by many unseen helpers. You are much blessed. We go now. Teacher."

Reading through this message after we had received it gave us a wonderful feeling of reassurance. It was clear and precise—we now knew exactly what we had to do. I must confess, I did wonder about the weather conditions: it could be difficult to perform the ritual standing in the open at over 1,000 feet up in pouring rain. Then I remembered the number of times I had doubted and the Teacher's firm reply: "Oh, Golden One, have faith."

On Sunday March 21st 1971 we walked down the wide green track leading to Tripp Farm, which lies on high ground close to Raleigh's Cross. Soon we saw the barrow standing out against the skyline and completely surrounded by ploughed land. After careful examination of the map we found that the exact centre of the contour was at the side of the wide green track and opposite the barrow. Here, at precisely 12 noon, facing magnetic North —which we found by using Dudley's pocket compass—we performed the first ceremonial ritual of the solar ray work. We were indeed surrounded by unseen helpers and received a sensation of tremendous exhilaration and joy.

The weather was clear and bright, and the March sunshine lit up a pale blue sky full of scudding white clouds. The breeze was fresh and gentle. We had the feeling of being much higher than we really were. The views around were wide and open, and on one side we saw Clatworthy Reservoir far below us, the surface of the water reflecting the blue sky and the clouds. The silence was awe-inspiring.

During the whole of our visit to this wonderful hill-top site, we saw no other human being, but the atmosphere around us was filled with nature spirits who shimmered in the light as they worked joyfully at their appointed tasks around the trees and the grass, in and out of the hedgerows and among the tiny wild flowers.

Occasionally a raven uttered its wild cry, high above us, and sheep communicated with one another in a distant field. Small birds flew low, flitting in and out of the hedges. We returned home excited and refreshed. The weather had been perfect.

Seven days later, on Sunday March 28th, we proceeded as requested by the Group in their message of March 19th to Elworthy Barrows, a great open space with views into several surrounding counties. It was the most impressive site; its wildness lifted my heart. The sky above was a pale blue vastness, and the power and the energy of the place was almost overwhelming. A number of underground springs burst out of its periphery. One particularly strong one was known as David's Well. Another flowed down through deep woods to Combe Davey. Cattle and sheep grazed the whole area at will.

The stillness of the place enfolded us—I longed to be down on the turf, to become a part of it. But we had come to perform the ritual needed to prepare the ground and mark the spot where the solar rays could enter easily and clearly to balance the vibrations.

We found the centre of the contour and at 12 noon, with both of us facing magnetic North, Dudley read the Great Invocation in a clear, loud voice and I performed the blessing actions. The ceremony completed, we were contemplating the magnificent position of the barrows, when suddenly a herd of cattle, their tails flying out behind them, galloped past us as if infused with renewed energy and delight. Amazed by this dramatic event staged by members of the animal kingdom, we watched as they flashed past us. It was all done with such glorious panache and good-natured fun, expressing the sheer joy of living in such a wild, wide open space, that we sent up a loud cheer of thanks.

On our way back to the car, which we had parked in the lane near David's Well, we walked right through the herd, now grazing quietly. They took no notice of us but, looking back at them, I saw one gently lift its head from the grass it was grazing and give me a wink of recognition. Animal humour is very real indeed!

It was a wonderful welcome on our first visit to Elworthy Barrows. Again we saw no human beings the whole time we were there, and the weather was fine.

***

For the Summer Solstice ceremony on June 21st, the Group asked us to visit Treborough Common, a high open area beside the long straight road known locally as the Prayer Way (which runs from Elworthy Barrows to Wheddon Cross). We found Treborough Common on our map and located the centre of the contour where we would perform the ritual. Joan Tanner drove over from Street to join us in making the first triangle of our solar ray work—her first visit and a very important one for us all. Kay Poulton, who was staying with us, also joined in.

Joan arived at 10:30 am. After welcoming her we all sat together in the drawing room to have a quiet time and compose ourselves before setting out for Treborough Common. As we approached this common, I noted that it was another high, wide open space, with long views down to Watchet Harbour and the waters of the Bristol Channel. We could just make out the South Wales coastline in the distance. On the opposite side of the road I saw what is marked on the map as 'Wiveliscombe Barrow'—it lay in a ploughed field quite close to the road and not far from the entrance to Treborough Common. There was a similarity to the Tripp Barrow site. The whole wide open space of the common was pastureland where cattle and sheep grazed freely.

A surveyor's concrete theodolite mounting block stood near the centre of the common. The great open sky above was blue and cloudless, and a soft breeze rustled the long grasses.

We found our position and formed ourselves into a triangle, the apex facing the magnetic North. At 12 noon Dudley read the Great Invocation and I performed the blessing actions. It was wonderful to have Joan with us to make the triangle strong and complete. We worked in great harmony. The energy generated caused my arms to tingle as I performed the blessing actions.

***

On the 2nd of September, to my great surprise, I received a typed message from Clare Cameron (Mrs Burke) the editor of the magazine *Science of Thought Review*, whom I had first met in Margaret Forbes's studio in Burgess Hill, Sussex.

It really was a bolt from the blue! And it brought me a wonderful sense of joy in its communication, as well as comfort, coming as it did in the first year of our solar ray work. When I wrote to Clare to thank her for sending me this unexpected benediction in words, I asked her how it had come about. She replied: "I was sitting quietly by myself, thinking of nothing in particular, when it came through with such force I simply had to write it down and send it to you. Its importance impressed me and I knew it was something I had to do immediately."

The message was as follows:

August 31, 1971

"Tell her, the Golden One, how much we cherish and love her. Tell her we are working through her far more than she knows. We are with her every moment, in her uprising and in her downsitting. As she prepares the fruits of the earth for her friends we distil into them our essences of potent spiritual nourishment. We 'speak' through her words. Though others may only hear the speech, in the same way we let our living essences flow through to quicken and bless others.

She is in her right place, and light and love stream forth from Gauth House and its cherished and much loved garden. These rays will penetrate further and further, for Gauth House is one of our centres linked with so many others now. But it has its own special atmosphere, its own delicate yet firm purpose, and this we shall reveal more clearly in the future. Already we have made it firm and strong with her cooperation and dedication.

Let her never be cast down or deceived by any 'appearances', for a ring of light is round Gauth House and into it always we pour our truth, our love, our wisdom and our blessings. She is one of our beloved servants."

***

The Group requested us to visit Elworthy Barrows on September 23rd 1971—the date of the Autumn Equinox. It was a Thursday. Joan Tanner drove over from Street to join Dudley and myself. As before, she arrived at 10:30 am so that we could have a quiet time together to harmonise our thoughts before starting out to perform the ritual ceremony at Elworthy Barrows.

On our arrival the aura of the place gently enfolded us in its stillness and its strength. We walked over the short, cropped grass to the position we had worked out on our visit on March 28th. Here we formed ourselves into a triangle, the apex facing the magnetic North. At noon exactly Dudley read the Great Invocation in a loud, clear voice and I performed the blessing actions. The energy around us almost lifted me off my feet and I was very much aware of the unseen helpers. The power of the place kept us all in thrall. We experienced a profound joy in being there and performing the ritual ceremony,

It was a soft autumn day. A large flock of sheep steadily grazed over the vast area, eagerly seeking the various herbs which they relished most. Occasionally they called to one another, making contact and holding the flock together as they ranged over the turf.

Rooks cawed as they flew overhead, journeying to and fro on their endless flights from nest to feeding place and back again. The high, wide sky was lost in a thin mist. The surrounding trees stood silent and still like guardians of a very special place—as indeed they were. We walked slowly back to the car, reluctant to leave this quiet landscape and so much natural splendour.

***

The date for the Winter Solstice ceremony fell on a Tuesday. Now that Dudley was in full employment with regular hours and responsibilities, he could not continue to take time off, so we consulted the Group through the Teacher and asked for advice and guidance. Dudley's position was accepted by the Group who then said that we could hold the ceremony on the Saturday or Sunday *before* the exact date. It would be all right because the energy built up during our performance of the ritual ceremony would remain potent in its own magnetic field, marking the Light point where the rays could enter on the exact date and at the exact time. This built-up energy was used up by the rays as they entered Earth's atmosphere—hence the importance of holding the ceremony before the exact date. If, however, the date of the quarterly Light ceremony fell on a Saturday or Sunday, so much the better!

This advice we continued to follow until the completion of the work in 1982—in fact, it enabled many people to join us who could not have come on a weekday.

Joan Tanner could not join us for the Winter Solstice ceremony because of a long-promised previous engagement. So on Sunday December 19th 1971 (the Sunday before the exact Winter Solstice date) Dudley and I, as requested by the Group, visited the tumulus which lay in a field close to the Prayer Way. Its exact position was in the corner of the field which runs up to the end of

Brown's Lane, where it joins Prayer Way. It was a corner site of great importance at the junction of two ancient trackways.

We entered the field through the gate and walked towards the tumulus which was covered with beautiful tall trees whose trunks and branches formed a graceful canopy. Its sheer dignity and stately appearance caused us to feel awe and wonder, and we paused and admired it before approaching. Carefully we mounted the tumulus, threading our way through the trees to the centre of the mound. Here we stood and marvelled at the intricate weaving of the many branches as they grew towards the crown of this natural canopy. With the compass we found our bearings and faced magnetic North. At noon, as Dudley read the Great Invocation and I performed the blessing actions, my arms blended in with the branches of the trees and I felt their steady energy flowing through me. It was strong and benign—this tumulus was a very special place, close to the earth and conducting the energy with a pure force. The vibrations were perfectly balanced: here the cosmic rays and the Earth's energy would fuse with perfect harmony.

The day was bitterly cold with a strong north-east wind. Occasionally a fitful streak of sunlight broke through the leaden sky. It was deep winter and close to the shortest day of the year as we stood listening to the wind blowing through the bare branches of the trees.

The sound was like waves falling on the seashore. As we listened, the peace and gentleness of this ancient place welcomed us. We felt very much 'at home' on this tumulus where we had just completed our first year of solar work in cooperation with the Group of unseen helpers.

1972

The Group requested us to hold the Vernal Equinox ritual ceremony at a high place named Lype Hill.

We found it on the map. It lay just off the Prayer Way, by Heath Poult crossroads, on the edge of the Brendon Hills where they blend in with Exmoor.

On the map Lype Hill appeared to be a high, wide open area of scrubland, dense and uncultivated. I looked at the map for a long time and then I asked the Group: "Please will you confirm that I have received the name of the Vernal Equinox venue correctly."

Their answer was as follows:

"Yes, you have received it correctly. The Light point we asked you to visit is Lype Hill. Here you will be met by the powers who control the solar rays. They will bring the important confirmation of your cooperation, which is proving very helpful to us all. You will be helping to reactivate this Light point. The ground will be cleansed and the energies of the solar rays will spread over into the Welsh lands. They will also spread out over the waters of the Channel dividing your two countries. This energy is much needed to restore balance and harmonise the vibrations. God bless you. Teacher."

On Sunday March 19th Joan Tanner joined us. After a quiet time together in Gauth House we drove to Lype Hill. We left the car in the lane near Heath Poult crossroads and walked through the dilapidated old farm gate set in a wild hedge, obviously uncared for over many years, and found ourselves facing a vast area of scrubland. Fox, badger and rabbit tracks created a maze-like effect. It took us quite a while to find our way to the right place, which proved to be a small, closely-cropped pasture on the crown of the hill. Here, after carefully checking the compass for the magnetic North and the map for contours, we formed ourselves into a triangle. As we stood awaiting the stroke of mid-day, a glorious stillness surrounded us. No sound came from earth or sky. The absolute stillness was like a benediction. At noon exactly, Dudley read the Great Invocation and as he uttered the words they gently melted into the stillness. Performing the blessing actions, I felt a great heat flowing between my hands as they formed the chalice above my head. The heat continued to flow as I brought my arms down into the horizontal position with my right palm facing upwards and my left palm facing downwards into the earth. The heat remained until the ritual was complete. We continued standing in the shape of a triangle, silently absorbing the love and the peace as well as the ecstasy all around us. Contact had been made. We had indeed been met and silently blessed by the powers who control the solar rays.

Dudley's annual two weeks' holiday from his office commenced on June 19th, so we could hold the Summer Solstice ceremony on the correct date, June 21st. As requested by the Group, our venue was to be Elworthy Barrows. This pleased me very much—it was such a magical place.

Joan Tanner drove over from Street and we had our quiet time together in Gauth House. The day was dull but dry, with a lot of low cloud all around which the sun occasionally managed to penetrate with a shaft of bright light. Summer days on this high ground often start in this way, gradually clearing to bright sunlight and blue skies as the day progresses.

As we drove upwards to Elworthy Barrows, the mist became thicker, giving the shrouded landscape a mysterious and forgotten look. All the familiar landmarks and long views were lost in the softly swirling mist. We parked the car near David's Well and slowly and carefully groped our way across the damp grass towards our correct position. The compass was invaluable under these conditions. The trees were also helpful, looming out of the mist like old friends helping us to find our way.

All sounds were muffled as we boldly set out our triangle. At noon we performed the ceremony—the sound of Dudley's clear voice was all we could hear. As the ceremony came to an end, the mist suddenly started to lift and the sun came pouring through. And then, to our utter amazement, we found a semicircle of cattle and sheep lying on the grass behind us. They had remained completely quiet during the ceremony and we had been quite unaware of their closeness. As we turned to go back to the car, they slowly got up, stretched their legs and followed us! The scene was like an etching by that wonderful pastoral artist Samuel Palmer. The little flock accompanied us to the gate and there bade us farewell.

The magic and the natural splendour of Elworthy Barrows had once again revealed to us the joy and delight which accompanied our cosmic work with the solar rays.

For the Autumn Equinox celebration we were asked by the Group through the Teacher to visit Treborough Common once again. The date of the Autumn Equinox fell on a Saturday, so again we were able to perform our ritual on the exact date. Our dear and faithful companion Joan Tanner joined us. When we reached our venue we found the common bare of animals and the turf which had been closely cropped during the summer months was dry and brown due, no doubt, to over-cropping and lack of rain.

The long views down into Watchet Harbour were misty as a pale haze hung in the air with no fresh breezes to shift it. The hedges around the common were full of spent wild flowers, fading leaves, rose hips and umber-coloured seedheads dangling on the hollow stems of cowparsley and hogweed, all good food for the over-wintering birds and small mammals. After a peaceful ritual ceremony filled with energy and light, we walked across the common towards the road where we had left the car. As we talked, we realised that we were now only three months short of our second year of solar work and the Winter Solstice would complete the two years. The patterning was taking shape. We were in harmony with our unseen helpers and our triangle was gaining strength.

The day of the Winter Solstice was bitterly cold. Frost decorated the landscape. Ruts and puddles reflected the light like mirrors and the ground crackled underfoot, hard on hoof and claw. The north wind came whistling through the bare branches of our trees, finding cracks and crevices in the Old House through which it could blow a cold breath to remind us that the shortest day of the year had arrived. We were glad of the Aga's warmth in the big kitchen and already looked forward to an afternoon sitting close to an open fire in the drawing room, the thick walls sheltering us from the cold outside.

Our ceremonial site was to be the source of the River Tone in the high Brendons. It proved to be a very beautiful place in an undulating landscape—a large pond surrounded with little hawthorn and alder trees shaped by the wind and the weather into dense and low shelter, much favoured by the sheep who inhabited the area.

We were now five in number for this Winter Solstice ritual ceremony. Our triangle was strengthened on both sides and the energy built up during the ceremony was very powerful. As we stood together after the ritual, I became very conscious of the elements and our dependence upon them, made up as we are from cosmic dust. It was too cold to linger in this beautiful place, so we hurried back to Huish Champflower. Sitting around the table in the warm kitchen, our fingers wrapped around bowls of steaming hot soup, we thought about the year which was just coming to an end. How grateful we were to the unseen helpers who joined us so faithfully. How delighted we were that the weather for each occasion had remained dry, as we had been assured by the Group through the Teacher that it would. We all looked forward to being together again in 1973.

1973

The Group requested us to visit Tripp Barrows for the Vernal Equinox Light ceremony. We were delighted to be visiting this beautiful place once again—it was the first Light point we went to in March 1971 when we started the solar ray work.

The day was bright and windy with clouds racing across the vast open sky. The fields of Tripp Farm were full of ewes and their lambs calling to one another and playing together. They clustered around the great barrows which stood out sharply against the skyline. The energy of spring was very apparent in the surrounding fields, hedgerows and trees.

Our ritual ceremony was a joyful one: just Joan Tanner, Dudley and myself were on Tripp Hill, but the surrounding Group of unseen helpers was certainly greater than usual. This made me very happy and enhanced the feeling of being part of the whole which is so essential when undertaking cosmic work. The pure spirit of nature, Pan, and all his subjects, his beloved elementals, were very close to us on Tripp Hill. I welcomed them all—their help was so vital to the well-being of the land. Their love, so readily given if asked for, was powerful for good in the surrounding area. I made a strong request for their help and cooperation to continue—and said, "Thank you all."

We were requested by the Group to visit Elworthy Barrows for the Summer Solstice Light ceremony.

Joan and I were on our own as Dudley was away (this was the only ceremony he missed in 12 years). After our quiet time in Gauth House, the journey to Elworthy Barrows was swiftly accomplished in Joan's big car. We parked it as usual near David's Well.

The day was quiet and the atmosphere remarkably still and clear. No breeze stirred the leaves on the trees; even the heads of the long grasses hung limply on their upright stalks. There was no movement anywhere. As we walked across the pasture towards our appointed place, the delicate scent of the wild herbs wafted up and enfolded us. The ravens and other birds flew lazily overhead, making fascinating patterns on the wide expanse of the sky. The stillness was intense—our every movement was recorded on the atmosphere and the smallest sound was clearly audible. It made us move very carefully and keep very still before we performed the ritual ceremony at noon. There seemed to be an air of expectancy all around us. It was a beautiful experience. The Grecian link became very vivid and powerful, strengthening the bond between us.

At noon Joan read the Great Invocation in clear tones and I performed the blessing actions. My body tingled from head to toe as the energy passed through me.

Joan and I had a quiet and joyous day together and parted with the shared feeling that the solar work was indeed progressing well.

Our venue for the Autumn Equinox ceremony was one we had not visited before. It was Heydon Hill, a very beautiful place not far from Gauth House. It was high ground above the fast-flowing river Tone. The whole area was heavily wooded with a great variety of broad-leaved trees, and shrubs also abounded. Brambles and whortleberries made a dense undergrowth, while gorse flourished with bracken and a vast number of grasses, rushes and mosses—a veritable fairyland!

Our appointed place was in a large field on the crown of the hill. This field was surrounded by tall beech trees on one side and coppices of mixed hazel, alder and rowan on two other sides. The fourth side bordered the lane leading to Chipstable and the long beech avenues.

We approached the field by a track through the woods and entered by a gate set between two giant beech trees in full foliage, their branches extending into the field, creating welcome shade for any grazing animals. The gentle strength and beauty of these giant trees gave the effect of entering an arena through magnificent portals. Sunlight flooded the field; brilliance was everywhere. Shafts of sunlight shone through the trees making fascinating patterns of light and shade. It was a truly joyful place. As we carefully located the exact spot for the ceremony, I felt the spirit of the place welcoming us with a quiet understanding of why we were there.

For this Autumn Equinox Light ceremony we were seven in number. Our triangle was steadily growing larger and stronger. During the ceremony a strong energy 'build-up' took place. Here the solar rays would indeed be able to enter faultlessly and accomplish their task.

The Winter Solstice, our last quarterly Light ceremony for the year 1973, arrived with bright sunshine, although the temperature of the atmosphere was rather low and we were glad of a warm house. Members arrived punctually to enjoy a quiet time of preparation together in Gauth House.

Our venue was once again to be the source of the River Tone, the same place we first visited in the winter of 1972. Together we drove through the winter landscape to the river source, eager to perform the ceremony in such beautiful sunshine.

As we started to walk towards our appointed place, a glorious sight met our gaze—a pale blue sky, cloudless and remote, the pale green vegetation around the pond, the sheep lying in little clusters under the branches of the hawthorn and alder trees, the sparkle of frost on twigs and branches: all created a scene of dreamlike, pastoral simplicity and splendour, dramatically lit by brilliant sunshine. It was breathtaking in its glorious naturalness and we stood gazing silently, lost in wonder. The artists among us expressed their appreciation of such an unexpected glimpse of a timeless pastoral scene. Once again I realised the joy and the delight which accompanied our cosmic work with the solar rays.

Our ceremony at noon was performed in perfect harmony and dedicated concentration. Our unity was complete. We returned to the Old House feeling refreshed and fulfilled. We enjoyed a very special meal together in the old kitchen with wine and laughter flowing freely.

Silently I expressed a profound 'thank you' to the Group of unseen helpers and gratitude for the marvellous weather. Once again I apologised for my previous doubts, their worthlessness now clearly confirmed!

And so ended our third year.

***

The way in which others came to join our triangle and share in the quarterly Light ceremonies was very interesting.

Elizabeth Burney was one of the Cove Rosicrucians. She was a trained dancer who, in later years after marriage and the birth of a son and a daughter, concentrated on developing her skills as a painter of landscapes and local activities such as Bampton Fair and the Morris dancers of Somerset. She and her family lived at Enmor Castle near Bridgewater.

Helen Clark, who lived in Street near Glastonbury, was a wise and knowledgeable Quaker with an open mind. Her good influence spread far and wide. She was the mother of two sons and had many grandchildren.

Elizabeth Fairclough was a member of the Soil Association and made contact with us when Dudley was secretary of the West Somerset Soil Association. She was then living on the Isle of Mull but was anxious to move to Somerset. We found her a cottage on Huish Moor and she joined us for the quarterly Light ceremonies early in 1974.

Barbara Crump we first met when she came to give the West Somerset Soil Association a talk on 'The Wheel of Life'. Barbara was an experienced ley-line worker who had written many interesting articles on the subject.

Joan brought her cousin Daphne and her old friend Enid Griffiths, an experienced astrologer with a wonderful sense of humour and tremendous vitality.

Christopher Newman was a local 'hippie' who came to me in the garden. He had great aspirations and was very sensitive. An orphan who had been looked after by monks in a Dorset abbey, he was trained as a nurse and that was how he had earned his living.

Derek and Jacqueline Randel lived in Wells. They were members of 'World Goodwill'. After a while they left us to go and live in Spain.

John Hall first came to visit me at Evelyn Heathfield's suggestion. He was interested in having a question-and-answer session. He was the founder of the very successful Helios Book Service, which he ran for many years from his home in Toddington, Gloucestershire, and his business had a worldwide reputation for integrity and prompt service. He was a joy to work with —very sensitive and very artistic with a beautifully vibrant voice. He became interested in our solar ray work, joining us in 1976. As he came from such a distance, he always stayed the night with us. This allowed us to have wonderful conversations in the evenings and over breakfast the following day. His loyalty and generous help have supported us in a truly fraternal way. Three of his delightful oil paintings decorate the walls of Gauth House. We are very grateful.

In the early years of the work, Kay Poulton often came to stay and join in the ceremonies.

Margaret Atkinson also came from Sussex to stay with us when the ceremonies were due to take place.

Once Mary Swainson came with Helen Clark, with whom she was staying. Mary's father had been rector at Langford Budville, about eight miles from Huish Champflower, and Mary had spent her youth there.

Joan Cooper from Culbone near Porlock came once before she died. Her sanctuary was in the most beautiful surroundings and in this place she helped people and wrote her books. She played the organ in the tiny Culbone church which she dearly loved and in whose graveyard she is now buried.

I met Leslie Godfrey on the train travelling between Bristol and Taunton. We got into conversation and by the time he left the train at Burnham on Sea I had asked him to come and have lunch with us the following Saturday! He was a very noble soul, generous to a fault, always ready to help others and his spiritual energy was powerful for good. His wife Vanessa and his two daughters, Meriel and Alethea, also joined us.

Dr Helene van Woeleren Koppejan we first met in Glastonbury in the early 70s. She and her husband, Willem, came from

Holland to live there. Willem was very interested in the solar ray work. We lost touch with them until 1980 when Helen Clark brought Helene, now widowed, over to join us. Stanley Messenger of the Gateway Trust also came with them.

In September 1980 we met Howard Davis and his wife Isobel. They lived in Milverton. Howard was an experienced mapmaker. Isobel was skilled at many handicrafts. They were most helpful with the final stages of the solar ray work.

At the bottom of Combe Davey—the Valley of Vision—there stood an old house close to a fast-flowing stream. Here dwelt two lay brothers, John and Francis, who maintained a tiny chapel within the house where a sanctuary light continually burned and where they sang the offices of the day. They cultivated their five acres of land, had a flourishing vegetable garden and kept goats, ducks, chickens and several sheep. From the terrace around the house there was a beautiful long view down the valley. John and Francis were members of the Soil Association and were very interested in our work. Although they never attended a ceremony, they seemed to appreciate and understand what we were doing. One summer they invited us all to tea in their beautiful garden. It was a perfect day, warm and sunny. We delighted in walking around their little estate and meeting the animals. After tea we all filed into the tiny chapel and the brothers sang their pure plainchants. In a timeless way we were transported back into past centuries when many monks lived in the Brendon Hills serving the local population. The peace in the little chapel and the surrounding countryside filled my heart with pure joy. We were indeed all part of the whole.

Chapter 7
The Group's Messages 1974-1982

In January 1974 the Group, through the Teacher, made it clear to me that the solar ray work (in the form of the quarterly Light ceremonies) was indeed progressing well.

They thanked me for recording the first three years' work with my own words, which they accepted as a true account of what took place. They then continued with the following:

"Now that our joint work pattern is firmly established and other people are joining our triangle by sharing the quarterly Light ceremonies with us all, would you, Golden One, be willing to record with your pen the messages that we wish to convey to all those present at each quarterly Light ceremony? The message is to be read out loud to the assembled company in Gauth House before starting out to the chosen Light point.

At the end of each year these messages are to be carefully stored in Gauth House, together with all the other messages received over the year from the Group through the Teacher. Eventually, when the solar ray work is accomplished, this material will become a complete record, from start to finish, of all that has taken place, and how it began and why. This full record will enable those interested in working with the cosmic forces to become fully aware of the work undertaken over aeons of time in the Brendon Hills area of Somerset and elsewhere.

We ask you, Golden One, are you willing to undertake this task? We know that you have the ability to do it but we must ask and receive an answer."

I thought carefully. I realised it would be a long task requiring concentration and self-discipline. I also knew that it was a task I could do and would do, gladly. My answer to the Group was as follows:

"Yes, I will undertake the task and do it to the best of my ability. I thank you for your trust and your cooperation. So be it."

In accordance with my promise, I recorded the Group's messages from March 1974 until the completion of the work in December 1982. These regular and detailed messages constitute a complete record of all the work undertaken during that period.

The frequent references to the ritual used during the Light ceremonies are partly because some of the people who joined us were attending the ceremony for the first time, and partly as a means of instructing us all regarding changes in the structure of the ritual as the work progressed.

* * *

"Welcome to all those who are partaking in this solar ceremony of the Spring Equinox. Together we are working towards light, harmony and fertility—three essentials for the progress of the human race and the well-being of all life on Planet Earth. Your work over the past three years has indeed borne fruit.

The vibrations in your area are very powerful so we ask you to use them with God-like care. Your work, simple as it may appear on the surface, is very far-reaching and carries great power. You are a unit in a vast project and, as you know, each unit is vital to the whole. You are also using the written words in cooperation with Pan and his elemental kingdom, as well as the animal, vegetable and mineral kingdoms. Remember this as you labour at your various tasks.

Your united cooperation is of infinite value to all life. We work with you as well as for you, and you work with us as well as for us—it is a two-way exchange of true love and compassion. As you give, so you receive: nothing is ever lost. The power of the solar ray is infinite. God bless you all and thank you for your trust.

And now to the venue for the Spring (Vernal) Equinox Light ceremony. Please join us on the Elworthy Barrows at our usual place and time. Form your triangle and after the reading of the Great Invocation and the blessing actions, turn inward and make yourselves into a circle with linked hands, then raise your linked hands and arms high into the air, *once only*. Bring them down slowly, unlink your hands and break the circle. We shall be close around you all. Be aware of the golden circle surrounding your group as you work.

Much good will flow from your efforts. Light will be able to radiate far out to balance the vibrations in the area.

God's love surrounds you. Now and always."

"We welcome you all at this most beautiful season of roses and sweet-scented herbs.

Please join us on Lype Hill at the same place where we gathered before. This Lype Hill is a very powerful Light point, so keep in harmony with all life and your thoughts positive for good.

Appreciate the natural beauty all around you as you progress towards our meeting place. Surround yourselves with positive love, and *listen* to the music of the spheres. Keep the living sounds pure. We shall all be close, enfolding and upholding you all. God bless you. We unite in gratitude and thanksgiving."

"Now has come the time to hold the solar Autumn Equinox Light ceremony here at the centre Light point—the Old House of Prayer (Gauth House).

Over the past years you have, at our request, visited the high points in this area which lies within your appointed place. This area of land you call West Somerset is indeed part of the whole vast project for cleansing the Earth now being undertaken by so many willing souls. For your faithful attendance, we thank you. You will be aware that humanity is approaching the climax of thought, word and deed. Much help is needed to keep true harmony, unity and the power for good in perfect harmony and balance. The pace is hectic and many could lose their way on the Path. Help from all quarters must be strong and held in perfect balance. This help is needed to resist the powerful magnetic forces working on a lower vibration which attract humans on the lower material levels: the glamour of things—the power and the greed to have more, to dominate and exploit all the kingdoms on Earth. All these dangers must be brought under control. We ask you to hold the balance clearly in your thoughts as Dudley reads the Great Invocation and Golden One performs the blessing actions.

Your centre Light point will be surrounded by a golden light. We will be present, close around you, radiating gold, silver, green, red and blue into and around the atmosphere to strengthen and uphold you and your work.

As before, please form the triangle, face the magnetic North and perform the ceremony of reading the Great Invocation and the blessing actions, finishing with the circle, hands linked and raised high, just *once*, and then brought down again and the circle broken. This action is for the earthing of the divine power.

God bless you all, dear children of the Light."

"Welcome once again at the ending of another year. Much has been accomplished during this time. Much still to do! The pattern of the solar ray work is now well established; you have made the necessary impression on the various Light points. These Light points need the continuation of this help which you have given them, thereby enabling the solar rays to work towards their maximum ability in the appointed area.

Will you please, if you will, meet us at the source of the River Tone.

The waters of the Earth are in need of cleansing and protection. Much has been done by humans to alter the natural flow of the waters. This must be guarded against so that the element of stone can reassert its natural actions in connection with the rivers and streams—maintaining the balance needed to control the natural flow of water. Human interference and 'contriving' has reached such a peak of greed that real danger looms in many areas. Nature and its natural ways need a breathing space. People should halt awhile and reconsider their present actions. Please help this to come about by continuing with your part in this project so many are working upon.

Water is vital to all life. Without it all perish and turn to dust.

We will be with you at the source of the fast-flowing River Tone. In unity is strength.

The usual ritual please.

We thank you for your dedicated service. Your apparently simple ritual actions and words are more powerful than any atomic plant—remember this.

God bless you all.

Children of the Light, we thank you."

1975

"Wecome to you all.

The Vernal Equinox solar Light ceremony. For this occasion we ask you to join us on Elworthy Barrows. This area is the most powerful Light point in your appointed place.

Please perform the whole ceremony, standing in a triangle and facing the magnetic North to read the Great Invocation and carry out the blessing actions, then forming a circle by turning inwards and linking hands and raising the arms to their full height—with hands still linked—*once* only; hold them up for five seconds and then let them fall. Unlink hands and slowly break the circle.

We all bring you most hearty and humble thanks for all your efforts. Work on the project is gathering momentum. The power and the strength of love is manifesting on many earthly levels. New thoughts and ideas are gowing fast.

The full plan of the project is now in operation. You are now part of the whole. Your group is now surrounded by the light and love of God (as the Great Invocation conveys).

Please approach our meeting place with positive thoughts and reverence for all life. God bless you all. Your work will be rewarded with light and love."

"The solar work progresses.

Together we are slowly working towards a great change in the Earth's atmosphere. Not the old methods coming back into fashion but something more positive. A new awareness of how best to use present methods, sifting the good from the bad; becoming keenly aware of the power and the majesty of nature; creating a closer cooperation with the cosmos; becoming more loving and tender towards life; gradually lessening the desires of greed for self and nation—a slow progress towards harmony through balance.

God bless you all!

For this glorious Summer Solstice may we meet together between the two rivers on Heydon Hill close to the tumulus where so much activity once took place. This area was holy ground dedicated to the nature spirits and carrying the everlasting aura of nature. Here animals were happy in their innocence. Here men and women worshipped the creator and no killing took place. Fruits of the earth grew here in peace and were gathered in due season by grateful hands working gently with love and understanding: sharing all produced equally between humans and beasts and fowls of the air.

We pray with you for this atmosphere once again to come about among these hills. The use of modern methods, if done with love and true awareness, could restore the harmony and balance.

The usual ceremony please—the triangle and the circle.

In your hearts give thanks for the progress, praise the work done and rejoice! We love you all. Sweet are the fruits of unity and harmony.

Within each of your hearts the Light shines—the divine Light. We thank you for your steadfastness, but most of all we give thanks for your love.

Go in peace.

God bless you all."

"Welcome to all of you on the occasion of another solar Light ceremony. The Autumn Equinox—a time of great fulfilment and rejoicing.

In spite of many earthly setbacks the *essence* is good. Much dross is gradually being removed—a painful process for all concerned.

Somerset, our fair land, has had its share of troubles, but this is the only way to learn the priceless lesson of detachment.

And now, dear souls, to our venue. We ask you to meet us here in the garden of Gauth House, on the centre of that green sward you call a lawn. Here we will hold our beautiful ceremony. Here the rays will enter in, in full strength, to help you with your work. They will cleanse the surrounding soil, protect the animals and all life, all living things, even the worms. Oh, how they work to improve and feed the soil.

Your sanctuary, this old house and garden, is the centre Light point for this part of the project; it is connected with all the other Light points in your appointed place. This ancient house and its very wild garden, so long allowed its freedom to be a safe place for all the nature spirits, is no chance thing. It was intended so that gradually *you*, working with the nature spirits, can create a lasting refuge with a peaceful atmosphere, so greatly needed to further the work of balancing the vibrations and the elements —earth, air, fire and water—in harmony with cosmic laws beneficial to all life. No easy task! But we do assure you that the rewards will be pure joy and infinite happiness.

Joan/John, our beloved third member of this triangle, we salute you. Your faithful work and your regular coming is much appreciated. Love surrounds you. Your green way blossoms and is filled with fragrance and the hum of bees. All who help with this work are blessed.

And now to work. The usual ceremony please. The ritual of triangle and circle. Oh, what joy it is for us once again to be with you in harmony and love. Your strength is clear and bright. We bless you all. We thank you, everyone.

God's love upholds you all.

We will be very close to you as you work."

"Welcome to one and all!

The Winter Solstice. An important time for heightened awareness and careful reckoning. A time to look and listen and help to hold the balance of nature which is constantly being attacked by human greed.

Our work over the past year has indeed progressed and established itself in the area.

As you know, this is an area where so much positive and productive activity took place in the distant past when humankind still regenerated the earth.

This area now needs most powerful help and protection from the badly conceived plans of modern humans and their determination to see nature only in the light of short-term advantages; taking no long-term consideration of cooperation with the landscape and the needs of all living things. Water, so pure and plentiful hereabouts, is now being offered in an unlimited way to distant towns. This is most unwise as eventually it will alter the natural flow from the underground lakes, changing the structure of the soil and the surrounding atmosphere; upsetting the weather pattern—making wet ground dry and dry ground wet, thereby altering the balance of harmony so important to natural growth. Help is needed to balance these changes.

And now to our meeting place for the Winter Solstice Light ceremony. Please progress with care and thought to the source of the River Tone, where we have met before, but this time progress further along the lane until you reach a gate. Go through the gate and you will find yourselves in a small glade with an avenue of trees leading off it. Stand in this glade and perform the usual ritual ceremony.

There is a large stone (quartz stone) nearby; it stands on the edge of the lane which joins the Prayer Way at Sminhav Cottages. This stone is powerfully magnetic and when reactivated by your ritual ceremony will in time link up the springs in the area. This is important. The stone can increase the vibrations in the area and help to prime small springs when needed. Concentrate your thoughts on this quartz stone as you perform your ceremony. Your ritual ceremony will increase the earth energy when it fuses with the solar rays. This combined cosmic energy will balance the damage caused by modern humanity.

God bless you all.

Our little group has many unseen helpers, so do not feel that you are alone and weak. On the contrary, you have the strength of the quartz stone which can and will help to keep the balance—in accordance with cosmic laws. Go gently, do not try too hard. All goes according to plan. Much joy will come to your group and much expansion in 1976.

Together we salute you all!

The light and wisdom of love surround and uphold you all."

1976

"Welcome once again to the Vernal Equinox Light ceremony.

All these occasions are so precious to us here in eternity. With the passing years we watch your faithful attendance at each quarterly ceremony and we sense your dedication and your determination to accomplish your task. Progress is being made, we do assure you. However, there must be times when you wonder 'where and how' as you hear of one conflict after another taking place in the world. Here we see the whole picture—all the thoughts, aspirations and endeavours; these are the truly valuable aspects which will enhance evolution.

Free will allows all to do as they will, but some see further than others and understand that gradually some progress is taking place. We thank you for your positive thoughts and aspirations—they bear golden fruit.

We will be with you on your journey to Heydon Hill to perform the solar Light ceremony.

As you approach the appointed place on top of the hill between the two rivers, please be silent. Keep your voices silent but keep your thoughts active. This helps to build up strong vibrations.

For Dudley, may we suggest that positive thought for the balance of modern farming methods will be of great value. To Joan/John we say thoughts about all growing plants will enhance their beauty and their strength. To our Golden One we say expand your consciousness towards the nature spirits in this special place—they love to respond when asked to help. To all the others in the group, we ask for the continued cooperation which you always give so freely. Thank you.

At noon form the triangle with its apex facing magnetic North. Perform the usual ritual, ending with the circle and clasped hands raised once only. The reason for this is that the one upward thrust marks the spot for the solar rays to enter and fuse with the earth energy.

We are now linked as a group with many others, the most important one being in Findhorn, in the north of Scotland. Your contacts are getting closer. There will eventually be communication between you when the time is right.

Dear souls, we send you love and gratitude. This simple ritual which you perform so faithfully and with such integrity is a vital link, important to so many. It is an act of love and trust. The sanctuary of the Old House of Prayer and its garden is much appreciated by Pan and his subjects, the nature spirits, by the birds and all life in the soil. They find true refuge here. Do not *ever* contemplate making it a showplace—that would not be in accordance with wild nature.

God bless you all.

We will be with you on the hill."

"Welcome to you all.

This is indeed a joyful occasion. As the years pass, so your advancement takes place. Here we see the whole picture of the project in its entirety, as we follow with interest and delight the progress you make in your appointed area. Each ceremony we share with you increases in strength. Indeed, your efforts are progressing the project as a whole. Here all your efforts are accepted and used with love. No effort is ever wasted.

And now to our meeting place for the glorious Summer Solstice Light ceremony. We request you to hold the ceremony on the green sward which you call a lawn. Form yourselves into a triangle in the centre of the green sward for the reading of the Great Invocation and the blessing actions, and then create a circle with linked hands which you raise, *once* only, to full height above your heads, and then break the circle.

This time you will be able to feel the vibrations when the solar rays enter your atmosphere at midnight. They will be very strong. Do not be nervous; they are cosmically controlled. Their radiations, which are completely benign, will enfold and uphold this centre Light point. Today's ceremony will be beneficial to each one of you as you work. The unseen company surrounding you will be very large; you have so many kindred spirits here who love to join in and work with you.

And this time I, the Teacher, will stand with the Golden One at the apex of the triangle, facing the magnetic North, and join in the ceremony as she makes the blessing actions. This is a new and advanced step which I take. I come to make it clear to you all that our unity is absolute.

God bless you all."

"Welcome to all who come to partake in the solar Light ceremony for the Autumn Equinox.

We rejoice to see so many of you working on this project. We are particularly glad of your help because this vast project (of which you are a vital part) is attracting a great deal of attention and interest on many levels, both positive and negative. Continual *balance* is needed, so please may we ask you to be alert and hold the balance as you work the solar Light ceremony. Thank you.

And now to our venue. Please meet us at the source of the

River Tone—at the grove of trees on the little mound where we gathered together for last year's Winter Solstice. Our meeting here will increase the energy needed to stimulate the nearby springs after a very dry season. Pure water in this area is very plentiful in an average season. It is of great value to all life.

The words of the Great Invocation are in themselves complete but, because of the lack of rain this season, will you please invoke the element water as you perform your ceremony.

We will approach you along the avenue of trees which leads from the quartz stone beside the lane. We will join you after we have visited this powerful stone. Our united efforts and our love in action will balance the vibrations and restore the harmony in this area.

We thank you. Your cooperation helps us to hold the balance.

God bless you all."

"Welcome to you all!

Some of you have come a very long way to partake in this act of love. We thank you for your faithful service. Let us rejoice together as we tell you that the project has overcome many setbacks and undesired interferences in many parts of the island and that the progress continues at a steady pace. Slow but sure! Vast projects need continual help to maintain their balance in an ever-changing atmosphere of love, hate, joy and fear.

And now to our new venue for the Winter Solstice Light ceremony. We invite you to meet us on the small mound among the evergreen trees which lies above Combe Davey, known to us as the Valley of Vision. This small mound is linked with the Elworthy Barrows, the most important and powerful Light point in your appointed place (as we have already told you).

As you climb out of the village of Brompton Ralph travelling towards David's Well, high above Combe Davey, you will see a gateway leading directly into an evergreen wood which lies on your left-hand side as you make the ascent. Pass through the gateway and you will observe the small mound covered with grass on your left-hand side. Climb onto the mound and, standing in its centre, perform the usual ritual ceremony of triangle and circle facing magnetic North. Your task over the years will be to reactivate this important Light point. As you work, think of the animal, vegetable and mineral kingdoms associated with this area; also the elemental kingdom—the nature spirits—so vital to the well-being and harmony of this Light point. Thank you.

We send you thoughts of peace, joy and contentment. Light and love surround you. All God's blessings are yours. Use them!"

1977

"Welcome to the Vernal Equinox Light ceremony!

This Vernal Equinox heralds the beginning of a new cycle of rebirth in all kingdoms. It is a wonderful time of aspiration and endeavour.

Your colours are indeed bright and the music, the melody arising from the Old House of Prayer, harmonises with the sounds from the surrounding hills, woodlands and pastures.

May we all meet together on Heydon Hill between the two rivers. There we will perform our usual ceremony of preparing the ground for the incoming solar rays, enabling them to fuse with the Earth's energy and radiate out their healing rays.

Approach the ceremonial site with love in your hearts. Rejoice with nature and be glad. Fill your thoughts with joy, heighten your awareness of all around you. Radiate blessings to the area, blessings of true harmony and balance, love and compassion.

God bless you all."

"We bring you all a joyful welcome!

For this glorious Summer Solstice Light ceremony may we meet together on the Elworthy Barrows, the most powerful Light point in your appointed place. When performing the ritual we ask you to make an addition as follows: take with you two large quartz stones (they can easily be found locally—they are much used in walls and gardens; you have many in your garden and in your walls). Carry them to the site correct for the ceremony and place one in the centre of your triangle which becomes the circle and one at the feet of our Golden One who stands at the apex of the triangle. When you make the circle after reading the Great Invocation and performing the blessing actions, raise your arms with hands linked as you have done before, but do not when you lower your arms unlink your hands: instead hold fast to your neighbour's hand and circumambulate slowly in a clockwise direction until the Golden One's feet are now again standing beside the stone which was placed at her feet at the apex of the triangle. The central stone will be a guide for your circular walk.

The slow walk in a circle will, through your feet, act like a pencil in a compass and make a strongly marked circle for the solar rays to enter into and fuse with the Earth's energy, and then radiate out to the surrounding area to perform their healing and balancing work, controlling the vibrations. These actions of yours will add benign power to the area, much needed now. We thank you all for your loving service and your faithful cooperation. God bless you all.

The Old House of Prayer (Gauth House) is indeed well protected, surrounded by the Golden Light.

Light, love and divine power surrounds you all."

"Once again we meet for the Autumn Equinox Light ceremony.

We link with you in thought, word and deed. We share with you an awareness of the fast-changing world. So much quiet activity is taking place. Old truths and 'sayings' are being discovered and looked at in a new light. Old myths are being reassessed, questioned and sometimes found to be false or misleading. This is positive activity but it can be disturbing to some.

We rejoice with you as you go about your work in Somerset. The energy is being restored and purified, and gradually the balance is returning to your area. You are attracting many wise and powerful helpers who join you in cleansing and restoring the Earth's fertility through controlling the vibrations.

Please will you meet us at the source of the River Tone where we have met before, on the little mound which is linked with the great quartz stone, the stone of energy which we have told you about already. Take with you two quartz stones and perform the same ritual ceremony as you did for the Summer Solstice, the result of which was a very clear circle for the solar rays to enter into.

Thank you all for your faithful service. You have a saying:

'Great faith moveth mountains.' We can assure you that this symbolism is very true. May it urge you ever onwards.

God bless you all."

"Welcome to you all!

The Winter Solstice is a time of fire and cleansing. In this Northern Hemisphere it is also a time of hibernation and rest. Each season has its purpose in harmony with the ebb and flow of the rhythms of the cosmos; a harmony and rhythm which humankind, as the supreme predator, disturbs at its peril!

Together we have made good progress over the past seven years. The solar rays now have a clearly marked entrance into your appointed place in Somerset, the Brendon Hills. You have been faithful with us in achieving this channel. Now this channel, having been created, must be kept clear and bright by all of us continuing with the ceremonies and acting as channels, each one making his/her special contribution. In this way, the brightness of the Light will increase year by year.

We ask you to meet us for this Winter Solstice Light ceremony on the green sward (which you call a lawn) in front of Gauth House. The full ritual ceremony please, with the two quartz stones and the circle walk included. This full ceremony with the quartz stones will strengthen the atmosphere and allow us to come as you prepare the ground, and be very close to all of you as you work.

This centre Light point (Gauth House) is indeed becoming a meeting place of great value to the project. Many more people will come and help with all the various aspects of the solar ray work. Year in and year out they will come and go. This sanctuary will support and encourage them all.

We send you our loving greetings at this time of festival. May joy and love surround you all and give you strength and renewed aspirations to follow your known work.

God bless you all."

1978

"Welcome to the Vernal Equinox ceremony. We bring you greetings of love and gratitude for your steadfastness.

At this time of resurrection and true understanding of the reverence for life, we are particularly happy to be meeting with you.

Will you join us please on the small mound, among the evergreen trees, which lies above Combe Davey, our beloved Valley of Vision. This powerful Light point is preparing to accomplish great spiritual work for the well-being of man and beast. When performing the ceremony of the triangle and the circle, we ask you to pray for the two brothers, John and Francis, who run the Combe Davey sanctuary and for their land and their animals. The full ceremony please, Dudley, with triangle and circle and the two quartz stones.

The work you undertook for this area in December 1976 has indeed borne fruit. We ask you to rejoice with us in this knowledge. The sanctuary in Combe Davey is now established and may grow. Your faithful service has been of great value. All who work with you send their thanks.

Life is indeed sweet . . . . We unite with you in our praise and our wonder at the glory and beauty of nature. You who are surrounded by it can savour it to the full. We say to you, love life, enjoy nature and all its mysteries. Be filled with joy. God's love surrounds you all. Use it well and rejoice."

"Welcome to you all, our faithful friends and helpers. Once again we come to the Summer Solstice, the watershed of the year's progress. And to you all we say, in truth, all is well. Outward appearances can be so misleading. We see with spiritual eyes and what we see in your area is steady progress towards harmony and inner joy.

For this beautiful ceremony of the Summer Solstice we ask you to meet us once again by the source of the River Tone, on the mound in line with the big energy stone. The usual ceremony, please Dudley, and Scribe, do not allow your imagination to distract you from the correct ritual. We were amused by your forgetfulness, but please this time concentrate! Each one of you is making a great contribution towards harmony and joy through this ceremony and also in your own lives through this contact. Your unity will bring you all the sweet rewards of a job well done; both material and spiritual rewards will be yours. Take heart and be fully aware of your divine ability and your intuition, which can bring many opportunities of service and success.

As you walk towards our meeting place, turn your thoughts towards the light, harmony and joy of working in unity with all life. The combined light which you radiate will shine forth and help humans, beasts, plants and soil in this area. Your energy creates, blesses and protects the area. Thank you all. We shall be with you in close communion.

God's love surrounds us all. Use it."

"Welcome to you all.

The Autumn Equinox ceremony is with us again, this time of harvest and recollection, of understanding and acceptance, of quiet thought and renewed aspiration.

For our joint work we go to a new venue high on your Brendon Hills where so much has been accomplished in past centuries and is now once again becoming active.

Please meet us on Heydon Common, contour 1050 on your map. Approach the common on the Lowtrow Road and enter by the gate on the left-hand side of the road before a group of rowan trees. There mark out your triangle and perform the usual ceremony of invocation in the triangle, the raising of hands once in the circle, and then the slow walk round, clockwise, for the marking of the area. You will bring the two quartz stones and use them as previously instructed, one in the centre of the triangle and one at the scribe's feet.

This area, Heydon Common, radiates out over hills and valleys which are fertile and harmonious. We wish to keep them in this state and ask for your continued cooperation. Your act will be an act of confirmation, holding the balance of humans and nature in true harmony. We thank you.

In unity we progress and thereby the Earth rejoices. To each of you we send rays of love, strength and renewed endeavour. All is indeed well with your group. Your seven years of faithful work have accomplished much more than you are at present aware of. We rejoice with you.

God bless you all."

"The Winter Solstice, a time of stillness and spiritual rebirth. A time of unity and understanding. A time of mystery and wonder. Let us all unite as one family and praise God!

Together we have made good progress over the past year. The solar rays now have a clear entrance into your area of Somerset. You have been faithful with us in achieving this. May we continue to keep the channel clear and bright with our beautiful ceremonies.

Let us meet on the lawn in front of Gauth House and perform our ceremony joyfully in the knowledge that it will strengthen this Light point and all who come and go here.

After the ceremony, rest and rejoice: talk among yourselves, exchange ideas and aspirations, learn from one another. Gauth House is a good meeting place!

We send you our loving greetings at this time of festival and unity. May God's true love bring you joy and laughter, and renewed aspirations to follow your own known work.

May the peace and the stillness of the Winter Solstice surround you all."

1979

"Welcome to the Vernal Equinox ceremony—this time of starting afresh, of hope and longing; this time for the sowing of new seeds and the visualisation of the golden harvest to come. May the world's spiritual sap rise as strongly and with as much faith as nature's. The need is great; much harmony and gentle tolerance, true understanding and joy need to be sown in all lands. Patient and diligent preparation and careful attention to details will indeed lay the foundations for the golden harvest.

We will meet you on Heydon Common for this ceremony (contour 1050 on your map). This area is powerful because it has retained the beneficial vibrations of harmony and unity. These vibrations have affected those who work in this area and helped them to work with nature. This, with your help, we wish to maintain. The rays which you draw down in your ceremony will strengthen these people and their animals, will enhance the fertility of the soil and spread out to the further valleys and hills, bringing renewed hope and endeavour to those who cherish this Planet Earth.

We will be in close communion with you, working on the solar ray. This simple ceremony which you do builds up great power. Over the years the power has increased and your own vitality has also been beneficially affected. 'As you give, so you receive.'

We repeat those powerful words you know so well. 'Let Light and Love and Power restore the plan on Earth.' We say amen and thank you all for your faithfulness and your joy.

God bless you in your unity."

"At this time of roses and sweet-scented herbs we bid you welcome to the Summer Solstice ceremony.

Our hearts rejoice at your steadfastness. Together you are building a bridge of great strength, beauty and power. The rays can use this bridge with wonderful effect. You have cleared the way for powerful rays to enter into the Earth's atmosphere and cleanse and re-create fertility.

Now we ask you to pay particular attention to the waters of the Earth. Much damage is being done to natural resources. By continually building more reservoirs and dams, the natural working of water is being sadly wasted, and it will not be able to fulfil its life-giving role as the powers of Creation intended. It will also alter the climate in these areas.

We ask you, therefore, to meet us at the source of the River Tone, on the mound in line with the big energy stone, and there hold your usual ceremony. The entering rays will help to balance the effects of humankind's over-eager interference. After the ceremony will you please visit the big energy stone, form a circle around it with hands linked and then raise them once only before breaking the circle and returning to Gauth House to enjoy your Summer Solstice feast.

We shall be with you in close communion when you perform your ceremonies and also when you visit the Valley of Vision, our beloved Combe Davey, so faithfully cared for by Brother John and Brother Francis.

May joy and reverence for all life be with you all.

God bless you, every one."

"Welcome to the Autumn Equinox ceremony.

We bring you all thoughts of love and fulfilment, gratitude and understanding.

At this time of harvest on Earth we remember particularly all those who work towards its fulfilment. We also, with you, become aware of the spiritual harvest. This is indeed a time of joyful remembering.

For this Autumn Equinox ceremony we ask you to meet us on the small mound above Combe Davey, the Valley of Vision, to give thanks for the work being done there by the faithful Brothers. This Light point has great power for good. Your united help over the past years has indeed borne fruit of the spirit as well as the earth. In perfect balance the effects of this work will bring joy and renewed life to both humans and animals.

We rejoice with you in your work. As a group you are now very powerful; the vibrations are strong to heal all those who long for peace of mind and body. Contrive to use this power for good in all your thoughts and actions. We unite with you, one and all, and we give thanks.

The Christ Light enfolds and upholds you all with pure joy.

God bless you all."

"With each passing year greater power and precision are needed because of the increasing density of the Earth's atmosphere.

Our work of projecting the ray involves us in the most exact and precise measurements and for this reason we need your one-pointed concentration when you are preparing the site for us.

The ritual of the triangle, circle and stones has great significance, marking clearly the area of entrance for the ray. To create harmony, serenity, one-pointedness and concentration, may we suggest that each member of the group undertakes one particular task connected with the ceremony? In this way all will be able to concentrate their thoughts on the work and thereby create a really powerful and clear entrance point for the ray.

This work which you have so lovingly and faithfully undertaken has to be precise, exact and harmonious. We need your help and your continued cooperation. Rhythmic stillness and pure simplicity will enable us to raise the power of the ray.

Humbly we ask you for your renewed dedication. This message comes to you all with love and gratitude for the faithful service you have given over the past eight years.

May the light and love of God surround you and uphold you now and always."

Suggested allocation of tasks:

Read the message:	Helen
Lay out the triangle:	Joan & Margaret
Place the stones:	Elizabeth
Invocation & timekeeper:	Dudley
Blessing:	Hope
Guardians of entrance & exit from the site:	John & Leslie

"The peace and the stillness of the Winter Solstice surrounds you all.

During this time of the seeds resting in the womb of the earth it is also a time for deep thought and meditation by the human heart, a time to meditate on the meaning of that vital word *unity* in all its simplicity, mystery and majesty.

Lovingly we thank you for your renewed dedication to the solar work. At this time of violent change in the Earth's atmosphere, the four blessed elements send you greetings and gratitude. Dear and faithful friends, our combined unity and continued steadfastness will gradually bring forth true joy and fulfilment for human, beast, bird, tree, plant, flower and stone. Your faith, shining bright and clear, keeps the sacred Light points in your area strong and unfailing. Together we thank God and bless his name.

May we meet together on the lawn of Gauth House, the Old House of Prayer, and there perform our ceremony, each doing their appointed task with loving concentration. Bringing the Light down on to this point will help all those who come and go here.

Joyfully we share this ceremony with you in the knowledge of our continued unity.

May this beautiful festival of love bring you all much happi-

ness, mirth and lasting joy.
God bless you all."

1980

"Welcome to Gauth House!

Joyfully we come and join you for the Vernal Equinox ceremony: the ceremony of resurrection and rejoicing in this season of revelation and renewed hopes.

Many times we have shared this ceremony together, holding in balance conflicting but complementary energies. This, as you know, is our main objective and with your loving and devoted help progress is indeed good. Your planet is the school in which souls learn and practise this balance by experience. As in all schools, the lessons are often difficult to begin with but when well learned yield great rewards of peace, love, true understanding and tolerance. When you say, "Oh now I understand," the Light floods in and spreads outwards to all humankind.

Together we will meet you on Heydon Common (contour 1050 on your map) and perform our beautiful ceremony with the triangle, circle and stones. This area of the Brendon Hills is very powerful and hamonious; the minerals in the earth are many and strong, particularly the quartz stones, which act as conductors. The solar ray can enter this area with great precision and power.

Perform your ceremonial tasks with quiet and loving concentration. As we told you, rhythmic stillness and pure simplicity will enable us to project a powerful solar ray enabling nature to accomplish its God-given task—all the kingdoms we know and love working in harmony. Together we work towards unity, peace and true awareness.

We thank you *all*.

God's love is in you and all around you. Rejoice with us in this knowledge."

"Welcome to the ceremony of the Summer Solstice—this beautiful time of the nightingale and the honeysuckle, this watershed of the year's progress. It is with great joy that we join you to celebrate and perform the solar ceremony.

Your work is closely linked with many others on the planet and gradually the power grows and the balancing action brings awareness, compassion, unity and understanding. You have a saying: 'The mills of God grind very slowly but exceedingly fine.' This is indeed so. All work must be thorough if it is to be of lasting value.

The waters of the earth are being plundered most unthinkingly. We are concerned. So much careless use of and misuse of this precious fluid causes endless trouble and eventually deprivation for all life.

We ask you to meet us by the source of the River Tone, the little grove at the end of the green lane, there to perform the ceremony: facing the magnetic North and in line with the big energy stone. As you approach the site turn your thoughts towards the uses of water and give thanks for its abundance and its generosity, its beauty and serenity, its life-giving force. Together we will work for the good of all!

Your group is now united in eternal love—a most beautiful shimmer of lights and colours. It fills our hearts with joy to be with you all and to experience this shimmer.

God's love surrounds you and upholds you. Use this love for the well-being of all life. We are close to you."

"With great joy we join you for the Autumn Equinox ceremony—this time of transformation, when all life gives thanks and gratitude to the earth and its endless bounty. It is also a time to give thanks to one another for understanding and true fellowship. We thank you for your spiritual awareness as well as your physical energy.

We ask you to meet us on the small mound overlooking our beloved Valley of Vision—Combe Davey.

This powerful Light point, so lovingly reactivated by your group and the Brothers John and Francis, is now fully active. We can use it according to the plan. The Brothers' work is now complete and it is correct that they should leave, after the Autumn Equinox, to take up fresh work in another area. Our duty, with your loving help, is to continue to hold this Light point in the Christ light and use it for the good of human, beast, bird, tree, flower and stone. We give thanks to the Brothers and to your group. This unity has achieved, and will hold, the power in this area. The spiritual harvest is indeed golden and eternal. God bless you all. Your faithfulness and your inner wisdom keeps the Light bright.

May your own harvest be recognised by your higher self and acknowledged in your actions.

In unity and love we join you for this ceremony.

God's love is within you and all around you, now and always."

"The Winter Solstice, the beautiful season of fire and love. A time for cleansing and starting anew. For our Group, it is a time of especial significance as it brings to a close ten years of faithful and dedicated work. All rejoice with you and send you most loving greetings.

Over these years our work together has built up the power of love in your area. It now comes through very strongly and benefits all the elements which feed the earth and it brings new life and joy to all living creatures. Together we thank God for his wisdom, love and understanding.

At this time we ask you to concentrate on this Light point, Gauth House, centre of energy and dedication. May we meet to perform the Winter Solstice ceremony on the grass in front of the house. Here we will join you with joy and gladness, fully aware of the progress made and the love eternal which exists between you all.

After the ceremony return to the house and sit around the fire, that most symbolic element, to talk together, exchanging ideas and thought and plans for the future. Rest and relax as you watch the flames. Allow your intuitions full play and rejoice in your work of holding the Light.

May this season of renewed life bring you all the joyful awareness of a job well done. Light and love and power perfectly balanced, this is perfect unity. We are now part of all of you. God bless you all."

1981

"At this time of the Vernal Equinox, this glorious time of rebirth and new aspirations, we start on a fresh cycle of concentration, dedication, joy and unity.

May we continue to work together towards reactivating the energy points—the Light points—in your area?

With your enthusiasm, and we use the word in its true sense, the power of light and love will grow steadily towards the balance of microcosm and macrocosm: the perfect balance within which all life becomes fully aware of its divine potential and uses it.

Together we will meet you on Heydon Common to perform our ceremony with triangle, circle and stones. This beautiful and powerful area enables us all to work well and allows the solar ray to come through with great power to heal and protect.

When placing the triangle cord, please make each side of the triangle measure two megalithic yards, thereby ensuring that, if the number in the group varies, the size of the triangle remains constant. This measurement is important to our calculations.

As you work to be at one with nature, rejoice in your home on Earth. Acknowledge your divinity and share its blessings with all life.

With great love and gratitude we say, may the light shine, the light and the love of the Cosmic Christ, shine for all life everywhere.

God bless you all."

"Welcome to the Summer Solstice ceremony, this beautiful time of the flowering of the rowan tree and the glory of the wild rose. At this time of manifestation it is with great joy we say to you that you now have in your group one who has undertaken a long and dedicated training in the art of reading and interpreting the earth spirit trackways, and revealing their true and spiritual identity and eternal value to all life. For this very important work he uses the modern human-made maps. His intuition and interpretation are true and clear. We humbly seek his cooperation in the months to come in assisting us to reveal to you the cosmic nature and final completion of the work which you so willingly undertook 11 years ago. Your faithfulness and dedication have been beautiful and a great strength to us here. We thank you all.

And now to our meeting place for the Summer Solstice ceremony. Please meet us by the source of the River Tone, the little grove at the end of the green lane, facing the magnetic North and in line with the big energy stone. As you approach the site be aware of the wonder of water, its life-giving force, its purity and its cleansing powers.

After the ceremony please visit the big energy stone and standing round it with hands clasped raise them once and then break the circle; as you do this, love the stone and give thanks in your hearts for its energy.

How joyfully we send you this message! The Earth rejoices and so do we.

God's love surrounds you and upholds you. Use this love for the well-being of all life."

"Through the pen of this scribe we have a story to unfold to you, which may help you to realise why you are now helping with the solar work in this part of the Earth known as West Somerset and why you have all come together.

In what is now known to you as the Bronze Age you were all part of a group living and working in the holy place called Delphi. Your place of work was the Tholos of Athena. Here you danced in the circular dance of praise and thanksgiving. In the temple this scribe was a priestess who played the lyre, and others of you were also priests and priestesses with responsibility for the flowers used in the rituals and also the food, honey, cakes and figs. Others of you were in charge of the wine and the herbs. Together you were a group and this scribe was the speaker for the group, as she is now in your present group work. This information regarding your work was given to her and spoken by her; now it is written as you know.

Your group was knowledgeable regarding the Earth's energy and its uses. Much study was undertaken by all of you. You used this knowledge in the surrounding area of Delphi. Each of you had a particular talent and responsibility, which you shared. You were well trained in the art of recognising vibrations, and helped many people to improve their crops and heal their animals through the right use of the earth spirit trackways.

Your work was powerful for good and as a group you were in perfect harmony. The word spread and you became known in other areas. You were asked to go over the sea to help in another land. In sorrow you left the holy place of Delphi, because you knew the work must be done in the other land. By ship and on foot you travelled to this other land, which is now known as southwest England. Here you laboured long and diligently, but it was a difficult task. The weather and the inhabitants you helped were often cold and uncooperative. Illness took many of you before the work you set yourselves to do was complete. Some of you became weary and withdrew, albeit with sadness at a task uncompleted. The power was strong and the memory was particularly strong with this scribe, the speaker of the group, therefore we, who are part of the group, but not in incarnation, were able to contact her and ask for the work to be completed. This she undertook to try and do.

Through awareness and intuition we were able to direct your thoughts and memories. Through meetings and the recognition of familiar vibrations you all gradually came together again. Your work has indeed progressed so well over the past 11 years that we can see the glorious culmination of it, in all its aspects —your working with the Earth's energy, directed through the triangle and circle correctly placed, and our working with the solar ray, which through our measurements and contacts can be beamed onto the Earth for the good of all life. The harmony has been wonderful to behold. In spite of all earthly difficulties, troubles and weaknesses, the work has gone steadily on and the Arc of Light and Power is now established.

This is what could not be completed when we were all together on Earth in the Bronze Age. It had to be completed on two levels to become permanent and a power for good. Each of you has contributed to this glorious Arc of Light. Some of you have come for a short time, some for longer and others at the final period to bring the necessary knowledge and understanding to complete the work, this great work of creative unity between humankind and all the nature kingdoms of the Earth.

To Joan, Dudley and this scribe we owe a particular debt of gratitude; their faithfulness and trust over the whole 11 years will in a large measure enable the work to reach its cosmic culmination. Their memories and intuitions have been clear and strong.

This ends our simple story. We have told it without frills and in plain language because we know how well you all understand the underlying spiritual meanings and the profound Christ consciousness which has throughout made this work possible. Our many messages to you over the years have conveyed our feelings to you all. We are in complete unity. As the one named Teacher, who has the task of conveying the messages to this scribe, I thank you all for your trust.

May God's love surround you and uphold you now and always."

"Further to the story of the solar work which we unfolded to you, we now have this to say:

When you arrived on the southwest coast of England, you travelled inland up the Washford River track, and then walked across to Tripp Barrows. Here you were met and escorted to Elworthy Henge which was your work place. You moved about this area doing similar work to that done in the holy place of Delphi. The sites (Light points) you have been working on this time are the same sites that you worked on in the late Bronze Age. Your dwelling place was close to David's Well and within the aura of Elworthy Henge, this glorious solar temple where so many careful measurements were made and where so much ancient wisdom is stored. This wisdom we, with your help, have used to create the Arc of Light. Over the past 11 years the reading of the Great Invocation, the blessing actions, the ritual of the triangle, circle and stones at the various Light points in the area have built up the thoughtform in subtle matter and the earth energy can now become fused with the solar energy, creating a powerful and harmonious energy.

The Arc of Light, like an inverted bowl, will be able to contain the earth energy fused with the solar (cosmic) energy. Herein this subtle energy can be stored and will accumulate to be used in the physical world by the higher powers, as and when needed, for the balancing and the well-being of all life in this area.

Together we are entering the final and most delicate stage of our work. Your united harmony and pure concentrated thought are essential for the completion of our joint work. We have complete faith in your integrity.

On receiving this communication your human senses may express amazement but look around you, become aware of the constant movement, the continual balance, the power of natural law and the beauty and the majesty of cosmic order.

You have the ability to use the cosmic outlook. The rewards are in infinity, which is now. We send you cosmic greetings.

United we are, and always will be."

"Once again we come to the Autumn Equinox and our beautiful ceremony of thanksgiving. At this time of harvesting the fruits of the earth, we become very much aware of our own spiritual harvest; together much has been harvested and our work, our solar work, is nearing its completion. Each season has allowed us to join you for these ceremonies. Together we have built up the thoughtform at the various Light points, which will finally allow the earth energy and the solar energy to become fused, for the benefit of all life in the area. The wonder and the glory of this achievement is beyond human words to express. Through this scribe, the speaker of your group, we have given you the story of the work and how it has evolved over the 11 years. We thank you all.

And now for the venue for this Autumn Equinox ceremony. Joyfully we will meet you on the little mound above Combe Davey, this powerful Light point which lies close to the great solar temple of Elworthy, where our work, when finished, will be cosmically manifested.

You call this season 'the season of mists and mellow fruitfulness'—how right you are! The harmony at this time is particularly powerful and rewarding to animals, trees, plants and all minute life in the area. It is indeed good to know that the balance of this life will be maintained.

Our joint harvest is the Arc of Light. Rejoice with us in praise of the Creator of all.

Remember and be glad. God's love is within you all."

"The Winter Solstice ceremony which we perform together has deep significance for all of us. At this time of inner creativity, of the rebirth of the Christ consciousness in all life, we come together in Gauth House to celebrate the Light.

Your years of faithful service and trust have indeed been fruitful. The Arc of Light is now strong, beautiful and powerful for good. It is well protected and in perfect balance.

The contacts you have been making in these past years are now complete and in harmony. As builders of the Arc of Light your work has been long and done under guidance from plans not seen by you. Your faith in us has been exquisitely beautiful—we wish you to know this. We were shown the plan and guided you according to instructions received by us. Our combined unity has brought this glorious Arc of Light into being.

Gauth House, the Old House of Prayer, has been our joyful meeting place on so many occasions and will continue so.

Rejoice with us at this time of celebration of the Light.

God's love is in you and around you: use it for the well-being and evolution of all life.

Our greetings and love to you all."

1982

Message received by the scribe (the Golden One) and relayed to Dudley and Howard:

"As you know, the so-called Elworthy Barrows are also the site of the Great Solar Henge where all worked together during the late Bronze Age, and from where we have been working during the past 11 years, with the Group's help and cooperation. Elworthy is the heart of our work, and there our last and most delicate task will be undertaken with your help.

The Henge of Elworthy holds the secret of the power of the Arc of Light. It is the central triangle and its completion which we now give to you to measure and work with.

The surrounding Light points, which you have all been visiting over these past 11 years, are now in full working order having been reactivated by the reading of the Great Invocation, the blessing actions and the ritual ceremony with the triangle, circle and stones.

Now this surrounding power has to be gathered together in the triangle at Elworthy Henge during the Solar Solstices and

Equinoxes of this year 1982.

Here is a sketch of the plan (see opposite page).

Into each corner of the triangle place a smaller triangle similar in size to the one you have been using at the ceremonies. You will notice that these three triangles fill the sides of the large triangle at the Henge.

The central and fourth triangle is inverted and this means that the final completing ceremony is to be held at Gauth House, the starting place of our work in 1971; thus the circle of work will be complete and the three triangles with the central triangle of the Great Henge at Elworthy will hold the Arc of Light in perfect and perpetual balance.

We thank you for using your talents in assisting us to complete this work.

God's love surrounds you and upholds you now and always."

Plan For Ceremonies in 1982

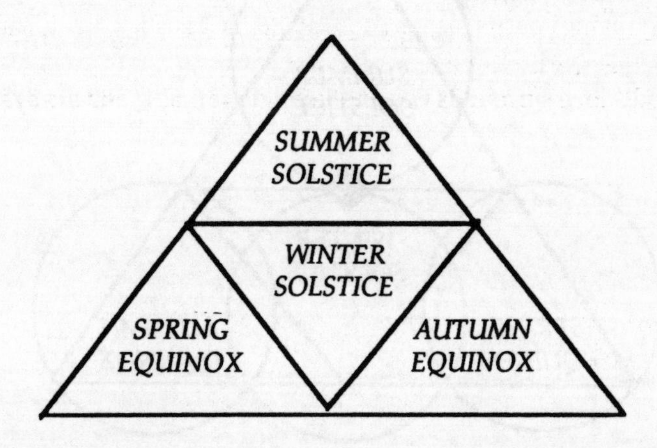

OUTER TRIANGLE AT ELWORTHY HENGE
(TEMPLE TRIANGLE)

INNER TRIANGLE USED IN RITUAL CEREMONIES

SCALE: 2 cm = 1 MEGALITHIC YARD

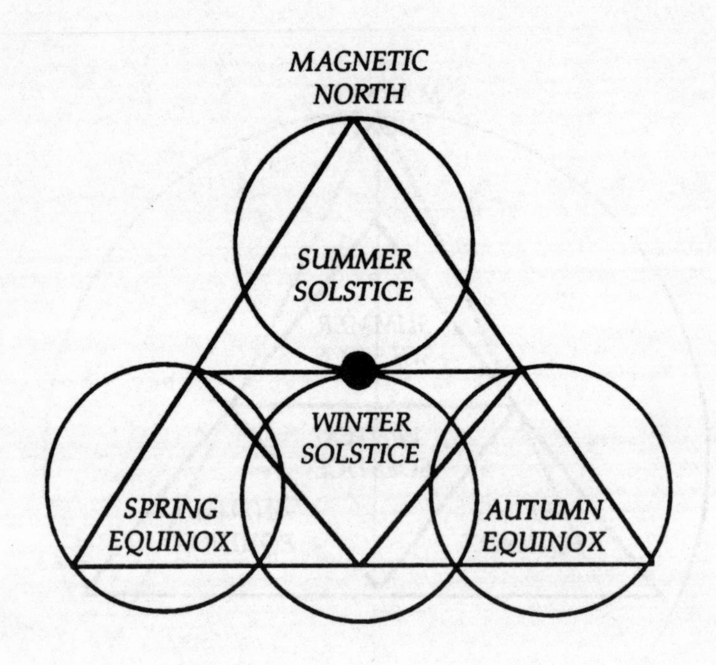

ELWORTHY HENGE TRIANGLE
(THE TEMPLE TRIANGLE)

CEREMONIAL TRIANGLE USED IN THE RITUAL

● OMPHALOS

SCALE: 2 cm = 1 MEGALITHIC YARD

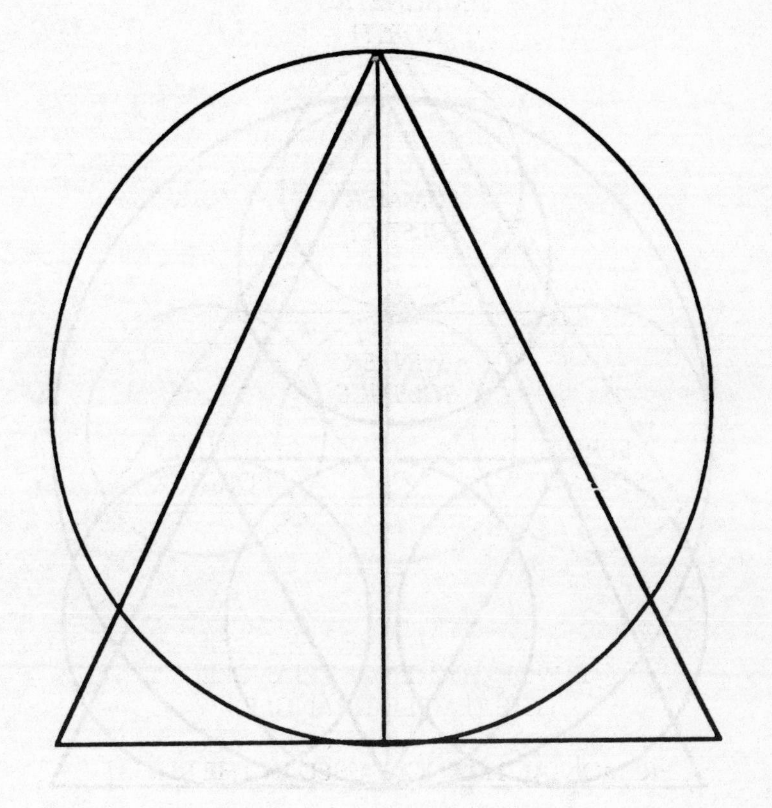

1 MEGALITHIC YARD = 2.720 FEET

A
B
D
C

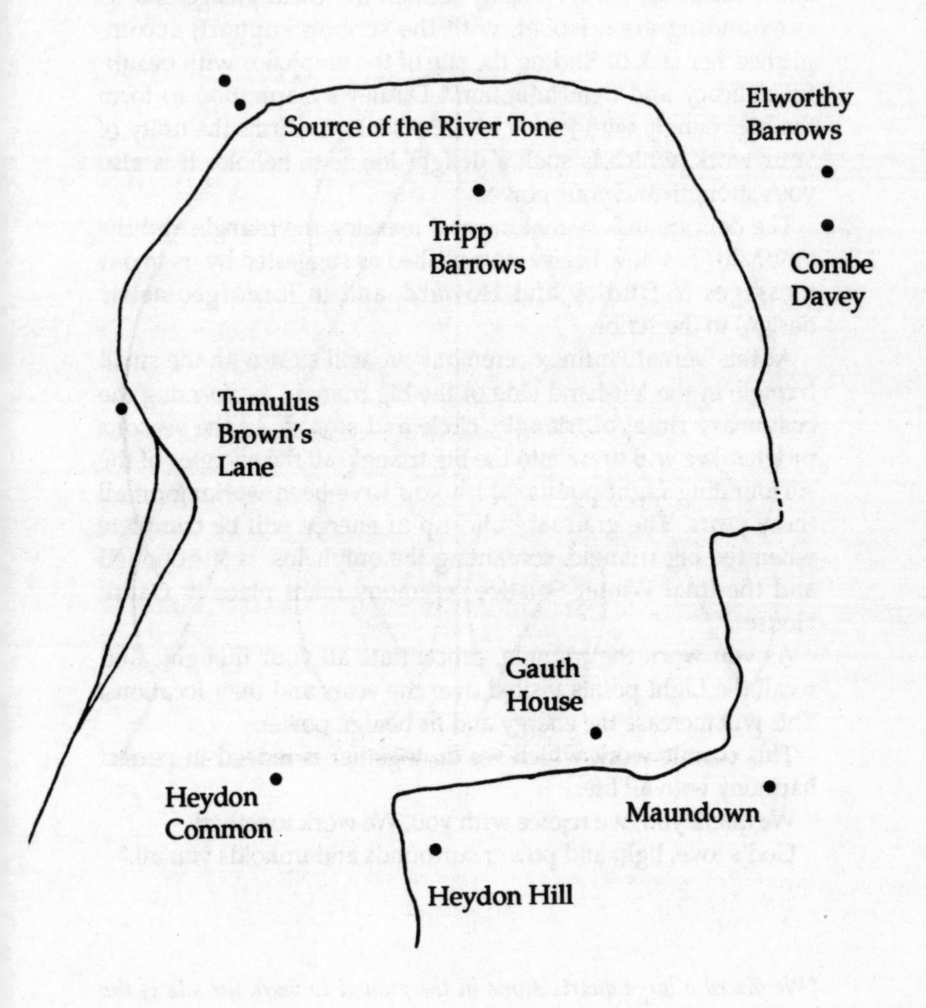
Lype Hill
Treborough Common
Source of the River Tone
Elworthy Barrows
Tripp Barrows
Combe Davey
Tumulus Brown's Lane
Gauth House
Heydon Common
Maundown
Heydon Hill

"Welcome to the Vernal Equinox ceremony which celebrates and confirms the renewal of all life in the Northern Hemisphere.

With joy and gratitude we meet you at the Great Henge, the sun temple at Elworthy Barrows. Here we begin our final work which will hold the Arc of Light in perfect balance into eternity.

How busy you have all been! Dudley's measurements, done with such eager devotion and precision, agree with ours. Howard's map readings, the fruits of much study, concentration and dedication, have correctly located the Great Henge and its surrounding area. Isobel, with the scribe's support, accomplished her task of finding the site of the omphalos with beautiful delicacy and determination.* Dudley's inspiration to form the big triangle with Joan's bamboo sticks confirms the unity of your work, which is such a delight for us to behold. It is also your strength and your power.

The delicate task of making and marking the triangle and the omphalos has now been accomplished as suggested by us in our messages to Dudley and Howard, and in form (geometric design) to the scribe.

At this Vernal Equinox ceremony we will start with the small triangle in the left-hand side of the big triangle, performing the customary ritual of triangle, circle and stones. As the seasons progress we will draw into the big triangle all the energies of the surrounding Light points which you have been working on all these years. The gradual build up of energy will be complete when the big triangle, containing the omphalos, is surrounded and the final Winter Solstice ceremony takes place in Gauth House.

As you work the triangle, concentrate all your thoughts and recall the Light points visited over the years and their locations. This will increase the energy and its benign power.

This cosmic work which we do together is indeed in perfect harmony with all life.

We thank you, we rejoice with you. We work together!

God's love, light and power surrounds and upholds you all."

**We placed a large quartz stone in the ground to mark the site of the omphalos (quartz being a conductor).*

"We welcome you to the Summer Solstice ceremony and bring you greetings of love, gratitude and joy.

At this glorious time of the earth's fulfilment, its energy is at its greatest and most powerful stage. This powerful energy will be drawn into our triangle as you work the small apex triangle placed within the greater triangle in the centre of the sun temple at Elworthy. Be aware of this energy and its beneficent power as you work your ritual. Draw this energy up through your bodies and then release it, upwards, to blend with the solar ray. This cosmic work requires one-pointed concentration and dedication, so once again we earnestly request you to concentrate on being clear channels for the energy, thereby creating harmony in the triangle.

Howard, son of Michael, has indeed accomplished, in pure form, the task we requested him to undertake last year. Through his work on the maps, in cooperation with us, he has revealed to you all the true nature of our joint undertaking. The figure on the map clearly conveys the outline of a perfectly balanced human head. The re-creation of this perfect balance will enable Glastonbury to become once again the centre of light and love which it was in the late Bronze Age, as you call it. Elworthy and Glastonbury in balance will create a harmonious and powerful whole, beneficent to all life in the area.

We wish you to know that your dedication and faith have re-created this balanced Arc of Light which we now see in its full splendour. Rejoice with us and be glad.

As you approach the great Elworthy sun temple, pause awhile and listen to the song of summer—all life humming to the glory of the one God. It is an exquisite sound, this union of heaven and earth. It is pure cosmic music and we long to share it with you.

We bring you our love and our strength. The eternal Now links us all in the love and the unity of God. Bless you all."

"With great joy we come to join you for our Autumn Equinox ceremony at the great sun temple at Elworthy. This festival of transformation will be our last visit working with the triangle, circle and stones, which we have all been performing with such care and dedication. The Arc of Light we have created together is indeed our harvest of 'seeds' sown so many years ago. The wonder and the glory of this achievement fills all our hearts with love, gratitude and thanksgiving. A service to all life in the area is now established on a cosmic level. The energy flows unfailingly. The fusion takes place continually, the balance is perfect. We ask you all to think deeply and realise to the full what has been re-created in this area of Somerset with your faithful cooperation. You have a saying: 'As you sow, so shall you reap.' Your cosmic harvest is indeed golden, true and beautiful to behold. Our unity has created this miracle. Let us give thanks to one another.

For this Autumn Equinox ceremony we work the small right-hand triangle within the large triangle. As you work we earnestly request you to concentrate all your powers and all your thoughts on creating a harmonious triangle. Feel the earth energy travelling through your bodies upwards to fuse with the solar cosmic energy. For the few minutes that you stand in the triangle let all other thoughts depart. Be clear channels, pure and holy. This work is very concentrated and exact and that is why you can only do it for this short period. After the ceremony, when you are back in Gauth House, is the time to talk and laugh and exchange news and ideas. During and before the ceremony we need all your undivided attention and concentration. These final ceremonies seal the success of all the work done over the past 12 years. Mental, spiritual and cosmic balance is delicate, precise and needs much energy.

Let us all work together. Thank you. Angels are all around you. You share God's love with all creation. We bless and thank you."

"To all of you we bring greetings of love at this time of the Winter Solstice. This will be our ceremony of completion after 12 years of steady work towards building the Arc of Light in your area of Somerset. Due to your integrity and your unfailing unity all has gone according to plan.

As disclosed to you in our earlier messages, this completing ceremony will take place in Gauth House, the Old House of Prayer, which is the home of the work we have been doing together. This final ceremony will link this most powerful triangle firmly with the centre of the large triangle in the middle of the great sun temple at Elworthy, thereby uniting the cosmic consciousness, in perfect balance, with human, beast, bird, tree, plant, insect and mineral. This perfect harmony and balance creates the Arc of Light, which now spans the area, radiating out protection and the power to heal. This cosmic radiance will gently and slowly bring unity in place of the conflict that has caused so much sorrow and misunderstanding over the centuries.

For this final ceremony please use Joan/John's bamboo sticks to form the single small triangle (size two megalithic yards). Place the apex of this triangle exactly facing the magnetic North, with quartz at the apex and in the centre: and the ceremony as usual. With the single triangle in this position the current of energy from the Old House of Prayer will flow directly into the central triangle containing the omphalos stone at the great sun temple—Elworthy—thus completing the work we have done together.

We give thanks for your steadfastness, your faith and your love. Let us rejoice and praise the Creator of all at this our completion ceremony celebration of the Light. The Arc of Light is now brilliant and its splendour is beyond words.

Now we leave you with the words which the scribe, our Golden One, has used so regularly as an invocation when communicating with us. These are words of love, purity and balance. They link us all together in cosmic harmony, joy and fulfilment.

'May the Light shine, the Light and the Love of the Cosmic Christ shine for all life everywhere and may the Golden Light enfold and uphold all those who come and go here.'

God's love is in you and around you; use it for the well-being and evolution of all life. Farewell to you all."

Names of Those Who Attended the Ceremonies 1971-1982

1. Dudley Tod
2. Joan/John Tanner
3. Hope Tod
4. Elizabeth Burney
5. Helen Clark
6. Elizabeth Fairclough
7. Enid Griffiths
8. Christopher Newman
9. John Hall
10. Jacqueline Rendel
11. Jacqueline's mother
12. Derek Rendel
13. Joan/John's cousin
14. Dr Helene Koppejan
15. Donald Starkbey
16. Leslie Godfrey
17. Vanessa Godfrey
18. Meriel Godfrey
19. Alethea Godfrey
20. Mary Swainson
21. Kay Poulton
22. Joan Cooper
23. Margaret Atkinson
24. Stanley Messenger
25. Howard Davies
26. Isobel Davies
27. Barbara Crump

	MARCH	JUNE	SEPTEMBER	DECEMBER
1971	Tripp Barrows 21st; Elworthy Barrows 28th	Treborough Common	Elworthy Barrows	Tumulus at end Browns Lane (nr Prayer Way)
1972	Lype Hill	Elworthy Barrows	Treborough Common	Source of River Tone
1973	Tripp Barrows	Elworthy Barrows	Heydon Hill	Source of River Tone
1974	Elworthy Barrows	Lype Hill	Magic Room, Gauth House	Source of River Tone
1975	Elworthy Barrows	Heydon Hill	Garden Lawn, Gauth House	Source of River Tone—along path to grove
1976 Great Drought Year	Heydon Hill	Garden Lawn, Gauth House	Source of River Tone—along path to grove	Above Combe Davey—Valley of Vision
1977	Heydon Hill	Elworthy Barrows	Source of River Tone—along path to grove	Garden Lawn, Gauth House
1978	Above Combe Davey—Valley of Vision	Source of River Tone—along path to grove	Heydon Common (contour 1050)	Garden Lawn, Gauth House
1979	Heydon Common (contour 1050)	Source of River Tone—glade	Above Combe Davey—Valley of Vision	Garden Lawn, Gauth House
1980	Heydon Common (contour 1050)	Source of River Tone—glade	Above Combe Davey—Valley of Vision	Garden Lawn, Gauth House
1981	Heydon Common (contour 1050)	Source of River Tone—glade	Above Combe Davey	Garden Lawn, Gauth House
1982	Great Henge—Elworthy sun temple	Great Henge—Elworthy sun temple	Great Henge—Elworthy sun temple	Magic Room, Gauth House

POSTSCRIPT

Ever since I agreed to undertake transposed writing with and for the Group through the Teacher, I have been the recipient of a very large number of personal messages from members of the Group—of which I am also a member. They told me that the Group is a vast one, linking together those interested in philosophy, science, music, art, literature and all aspects of the natural world, especially the elemental kingdom and the pure spirit of nature, Pan himself.

All the messages I have received were sent in order to help, advise and inform me. They have always urged me to make good use of my imagination and my intuition, and always to question anything which I thought incorrect or unworkable. I am deeply grateful and freely acknowledge the help I have been given. I have used only a few of these personal messages in *The Maze and the Arc of Light*, because of their intimate nature. However, there are some which the reader might find interesting or relevant so I am including them in this postscript.

Here are four short messages giving information:

1. "The Group of which you are a member is indeed vast—and yet each member's own experience is a vital contribution to the whole. Each member continues to research their own particular subject, and when the research is completed they share this knowledge with the other members of the Group. New discoveries are constantly being made and passed on to others to use as and when the time is right. This continual but gradual creation is cosmic consciousness in its truest sense."

2. "The words which we send to you are very carefully chosen by us. We do not promise what we cannot deliver. Remember this please. Between us there is complete trust and unity."

3. "You and your pen act as our link. Through your pen we can communicate with others in the Group who are presently incar-

nated in an earthly personality. Through your pen we can attempt to answer the questions put to us. We always try to help those who really want to know for a particular reason—not just idle curiosity, which creates a negative atmosphere and wastes valuable energy."

4. "Transposed writing, achieved through your pen, is of infinite value to us. It is the essential link. Completing the solar ray work in your area will achieve the successful fusion of solar energy and earth energy. This will be a much greater achievement than you can at present realise. It is part of a great change which has to come about. Cosmic forces *are* linked with human endeavour. Be aware of the power of the written word which lives on from one generation to another and carries the knowledge forward."

***

There have been many occasions when I have felt distressed and bewildered by the sounds of modern machinery, and by society's urgent demands for more and more mechanical equipment. After one particularly difficult period I received a message direct from Pan. He said: "Think of us. Withdraw and listen to the sounds of nature. Keep very still and become part of us. Work with us—we will help you. The animal, vegetable, mineral and elemental kingdoms all welcome you. You are *complete* with us. Be calm, you still have much writing to do. We all need your pen! Stand very still in your garden; the trees and the flowers will surround you. You are part of us and we are part of you. We all love you. Be at peace."

As I read through this message, relief and joy flowed through me. How delightful to know that Pan was so close. Later, standing very still in the sunlit garden, surrounded by trees and flowers, I gazed at a single golden marigold which I held in my hand. As I looked into its brilliance, I recalled this poem written by our dear old friend, the Scottish poet and painter Margaret Forbes:

Watching your fiery disc that seems to glow, igniting
Diadems of sun in sun delighting,

I wonder what flaming petals crown me too, as I stand
Holding you, beautiful one, in my hand.

***

On December 27th 1982 I received the following message:

"We greet you.

Golden One, thanks come to you from the members of your Group now in eternity.

Now that the work with the solar rays is finally completed, our joy and relief goes out in ever-widening waves of light.

When you have rested yourself will you please consider writing the whole story of the solar ray work. How it began so long ago, in Greece and Bronze Age England. And how you finally completed the task with the help of the other members of the Group.

This information needs to be recorded for posterity. The link now forged between Elworthy and Glastonbury must be appreciated by those who come after you. Through your written words they will understand that the delicate balance which the Arc of Light creates is of tremendous cosmic importance. It is a continual balance between cosmic consciousness and the very real temptations of material greed which the Arc of Light now controls. This balance is delicate but powerful for good. Its harmony overlights the whole area.

Writing the story will be slow work. Carefully sift through all the material you have collected and take time to consider it well before you commit any words to paper.

Again we say thank you, Golden One. We all love you and need your help. Teacher."

Although the solar ray work which we had undertaken was sucessfully completed at the Winter Solstice ceremony of 1982, I still felt the urge to revisit the little mound above Combe Davey (the Valley of Vision). So the following year, 1983, Dudley and I revisited this special place in March and June (the Vernal Equinox and the Summer Solstice). I experienced the same powerful energy flowing through this 'junction box' as the Teacher had named it. After the visits I felt refreshed and strengthened and I was aware that our visit had been appreciated by the unseen helpers. When September came (Autumn Equinox), I questioned the Group through the Teacher about my intuitive urge to revisit this little mound above Combe Davey and received the following message:

"We greet you.

You were right, Golden One, to visit the little mound above the Valley of Vision. This close and vital link with the Henge will benefit from your visits. It is a very powerful control centre.

It is indeed the junction through which the earth energy, travelling towards Elworthy from the reactivated Light points in the area, passes. Here the earth energy is controlled and channelled into the big triangle in the sun temple of the Great Solar Henge, where the fusion takes place, creating the Arc of Light. The Arc of Light is now brilliant, and the power is very strong, but so also are the negative powers and this always has to be kept in careful balance. Together we have achieved this balance over the 12 years, and it will continue so. We rejoice that our work has been so successful. Between us is complete trust and unity. Your visits are as a brilliant flash of light, illuminating the area.

Please try to complete the written story of your task. When it is accomplished it will make the most glorious pattern of a perfect ovoid—a joy to us all. The Group members here in eternity can now, through the completion of the solar ray work, progress to other work in the Light. The unfinished work is now complete and the Arc of Light is brilliant. Thank you!

We say to you: continue to follow the ways of wild nature, Golden One. Pan needs your help. The Light is all around you. We send you our love on all levels. Teacher."

In 1981 I received the first of very many personal messages from Roc (Robert Ogilvie Crombie), one of the people closely associated with the founding of the Findhorn Foundation on the Moray Firth in Scotland. His particular interest was the community's garden. I was delighted to receive this first message, but I was surprised! The message was full of encouragement regarding the solar ray work, about which he seemed to be very knowledgeable. I recognised his strong link with the pure spirit of nature, Pan. In his first message he wrote: "We have a close link with Pan, you and I. Please care for it and cultivate it. We need your continued help with your pen. Open your heart to me; we belong to the same Group. You are one of us. Your thoughts weave patterns of great beauty. Be filled with joy. You are indeed accomplishing the task asked of you. The Group here send you love and gratitude for your dedication and determination."

On another occasion he wrote: "*All is* going according to plan. Rest yourself, relax and remember that we are all close to you. Disregard those negative comments which other people make concerning cosmic energy. Stay positive and continue to be aware of us.

The elementals, the fairies, the nature spirits and the angels of Light all love you and work with you. Develop this awareness—make it part of yourself; its strength will bring you peace of mind. Your pen brings you so close to us. Share this closeness and awareness with others by writing your story—when you are ready to do so.

The Arc of Light is glorious to behold. We see it in its full splendour.

Our united love comes to you on rays of coloured lights—the main one is pure gold."

After receiving one of Roc's illuminating messages, I decided to ask him a question. It was: "Where are you now, Roc?"

There was a short pause and then the reply came as follows:

"In eternity. It is a state of mind, where all is possible. Where thoughts become actions. Where memories of life on Earth are sorted out and understood. Where reunions take place. The release from the human body is exquisite. We 'live' in our etheric bodies.

We link with those who are kindred spirits (in the widest sense of the word). We follow interests and resolve situations impossible to achieve when in the flesh of a human body on the dense Planet Earth (which is our most difficult and challenging learning centre).

The etheric body is perfect—complete and without flaw. Our thoughts express our feelings: music, colour, landscapes, buildings etc are all here, as are the four kingdoms. Their reality is clear to us. Here our Light bodies can penetrate and perceive that which on Earth we found so dense and incomprehensible. Here each soul follows its true vocation; facilities are available to all.

Travel to many different planets can take place in groups or singly or in pairs. The etheric body is composed of force currents and in it are vital centres linked by lines of force with each other. The etheric body is vitalised and controlled by thought.

When you on Earth talk to someone on the telephone, you cannot see them but your power of thought tells you it is their voice, so you talk freely with them. The human-made instrument which enables you to do so is also created by thought. We communicate with you in a similar way. We 'tune in' to your magnetic field and then fix the vibration which you will respond to (as you dial a number)—hoping that contact has been made. If we get no reply, or if we get 'number engaged', we wait and try again. If, after making several 'calls', we still get no reply, we then know that you are 'unobtainable'. So many people incarnated on Earth never answer a 'call'. It is sad but true.

And then sometimes you will make a 'call' and we do not answer! The lines of communication are always on the move —the endless flow of give and take . . . .

Does this writing of mine help you? Remember, life on Earth is a journey—your home is here with us. God bless you. We all love you.

The word 'love' is so often misunderstood. It has so many different meanings—positive and negative. Our love for you is positive and complete. Thank you for maintaining contact with us. Your line is very clear and strong. We *still* need your pen! Roc."

In the autumn of 1987 the Findhorn Foundation celebrated its 25th anniversary. In the anniversary copy of their magazine *One Earth* there were many articles by and about the founders and the community. Page 18 was devoted to Roc. It contained an article written by Ross Stewart, the first chairman of the Foundation's board of trustees, entitled 'Do you Love Pan?' There was a photograph of Roc and one of Ross Stewart among other Foundation trustees. There was also a short write-up about Roc, part of which read as follows:

"He was a wise man, a magician who worked with earth energies. He described part of his task as reactivating and linking together power points around Britain and was instrumental in grounding the community's connection with Iona and Glastonbury. He also introduced the community to the reality and significance of the ancient nature energies in the being of the great god Pan."

As I read these words, I felt the *fohat* (the strong electric current) run through me. Here, from an unknown source, I was receiving a confirmation of Roc's messages and the reason why he had contacted me. This unbiased information has greatly enhanced my appreciation of Roc's many helpful messages. My ungracious surprise when the messages first started to arrive has, I'm sure, been understood and forgiven by him, because 'in nature everything has a meaning and everything is forgiven, and it would be strange not to forgive'.

To my great delight Roc's messages to me still continue to arrive. I value them because they are such a wonderful link —full of wisdom and humour. He has constantly urged me to write *The Maze and the Arc of Light* and to share it with others.

When I finally completed it, he wrote: "Excellent! It has so much within it which is relevant to life on Earth today. Now that you have successfully completed your incarnation task, be filled with joy. Your Golden Thread of Awareness links us all together —we are all part of the whole. Cosmic laws are indeed God's laws."

Finally I would like to say a profound 'thank you' to all those, both here and in eternity, who have helped me. Your faith, trust and compassion have created the Arc of Light for the well-being of all life in this area of southwest Somerset.